The Essential Women's Guide to
BUYING A FRANCHISE

The plain speaking guide to unlocking your franchise dreams

Clive Sawyer & Murielle Maupoint

lıp

First published in 2013 by:

Live It Publishing
27 Old Gloucester Road
London, United Kingdom.
WC1N 3AX
www.liveitpublishing.com

Photographs courtesy of Steve Bishop Photography
www.stevebishopphotography.com

ISBN 978-1-906954-78-9 (pbk)

Dedicated to our wonderful daughters and the future
generation of women business owners

CONTENTS

PART 4 – USEFUL INFORMATION 185

FOREWORD

I first met Clive Sawyer when looking for a suitable consultant to help my husband, Peter, and I to franchise Peter's business. In 2010 we wanted to (finally) establish whether franchising was the right route for expansion. I had been a franchisee and worked for the franchisor as a trainer and with that little knowledge we thought we might make a go of franchising. We wanted to expand our successful small business based in Newbury but, like many people who ultimately franchise, had no desire to manage staff in, for example, Manchester with all the on-going challenges that would present.

Franchising is not the only choice, when expanding, and it's not the cheapest or easiest option. Personally, I feel it is incredibly rewarding to offer people the chance to be more. That may sound a little grand but running your own business is liberating. Hard work but fantastic. And buying a franchise is one of the best opportunities people can take if they are slightly risk averse and not an out and out entrepreneur – but they know that they want to be mistress (or master) of their own destiny.

I am now the Franchise Director and co-owner of Wilkins Chimney Sweep Limited, a 'man-in-a-van' franchise officially launched on 22nd December 2010. We could not have done it without the guidance and knowledge that Clive brought to the business. We also know that our subsequent success in the franchise market is largely due to the level of guidance and support that Clive provided then and since.

Franchising is an industry in its own right. It comes with its own set of suppliers, behaviours, characters, challenges, stories and legal grounding. I am not (and indeed never was) a chimney sweep – I am a franchisor running a franchise business. There are a fair few of us out there and we collectively represent a good part of the world economy through both our local businesses and franchisees.

What I personally love about the franchise world is the collaborative nature of the businesses that make up the whole industry. I am drawn to using a franchise whenever I am looking for a supplier since I wish to support my fellow franchisors. There are so many great examples of women who are a joyous example of how to do it right that I would (and do) urge friends, family and indeed complete strangers who are thinking about venturing out on their own to consider a franchise. There is nearly always someone who has heard the story or lived the challenge before and is willing to help – franchisors, franchisees and suppliers.

I first met Murielle through Clive when I went to my first EWIF meeting. EWIF (Encouraging Women Into Franchising) is a not-for-profit organisation that aims to support women to select franchising as an option to fulfill their business ownership aspirations and to encourage more franchisors to recruit female franchisees. Like charities the world over who represent inequities in life (from the tragic to the flippant) it is an organisation that needs to make itself redundant quickly. Murielle, a founding member and Director of EWIF, is a prime example of women 'just getting on with it' and not allowing the fact that she's a woman to stand in the way. I was intrigued, however, to find that, in franchising, women are underrepresented and hence why EWIF was created.

The only reason that I can offer for this inequity is that women lack confidence - which is fundamental madness. Franchising is a perfect business model for women! Buy into an established model and follow that model - maintain relationships with customers, clients, suppliers and franchisors – juggle the needs of business vs home life – deliver energy and passion into your business – the cornerstones lend themselves perfectly to the female psyche. So can it only be that women don't have the confidence to take the step? I'm not a true feminist by any means but have been brought up in an age when we had our first female prime minister and I have never believed there was anything to stop me, as a woman, except for my own attitude!

In 2012 I entered my first ever awards. I'd like to tell you that

Clive, at the time Chair of EWIF, encouraged me to do this but he didn't. A number of other industry related people encouraged me, I entered – and I won the EWIF New Woman Franchisor award. The overall reason given was that we had 'done it right' and the increased energy and enthusiasm that the award gave me is still with me.

At the end of 2012, Clive retired as chair of EWIF and left a huge pair of shoes to fill. In true Remington style, I put my hand up and was appointed co-chair of EWIF in September 2012. We'd love to make EWIF redundant by 2015 and this book will go some way, I trust, to making that happen. As any chair of a voluntary committee will tell you – obsolescence is the ultimate dream!

It is important that this book draws on the experience of real, and fundamentally 'normal', women who have bought into a franchise model and work successfully in the industry. I hope that women everywhere, who would like the freedom of being their own boss and running their own business, will access a copy and be inspired to take that step towards their goal.

I realise I sound rather evangelical about franchising, largely because of the opportunities and enjoyment it has afforded me. There are, however, pitfalls and challenges and this book goes some way to help people avoid those pitfalls and make the right choices.

My guess is you are reading this because you have an interest in owning your own business. I say to you – go for it. Look for EWIF on the web. If we are no longer in existence, you're entering an industry that is as welcoming for women as men. If we are still visible, we need more women to join us and progress the understanding that we are as good as any man and might just make a better job of franchise ownership than the next <u>man!</u>

By **Louise Harris**
Managing Director
Wilkins Chimney Sweep
Chairman, Encouraging Women into Franchising (EWIF)

INTRODUCTION

Having been involved in franchising and business consultancy for nearly twenty years I have personally witnessed and helped many people to start-up their own business and also to enter the world of franchising. The skills required to run a business are virtually always the same however the personal attitude and discipline required to start a business from scratch compared to running a franchise are often very different.

I started my business life in the early 80's at a time when it appeared that the only way women were going to succeed in corporate life was to adopt an over exaggerated male approach to the way they conducted themselves. This meant they were often very ruthless and insensitive to the needs of their staff. All the benefits that a female approach could bring to a business were lost in the striving to beat men at their own game.

Fortunately over the last three decades women have been better accepted in the workplace by their male colleagues and women themselves have realised that they can bring skills and benefits to the workplace that their male counterparts do not have. However in my eyes there is still some way to go before women are viewed as true equals to men. Hopefully my daughter's generation will be able to help make this final transition.

Franchising is no different when it comes to the way women have previously been viewed. Women are underrepresented in the world of franchising despite often being better suited to being a franchisee than men. Franchising is based on the concept of paying money to be granted the right to have a business whereby they follow a proven profitable model with centralised support. For many women this can be the ideal way of owning and running a business. Operating a franchise allows you to benefit from all the experience and hard work of the franchisor. This therefore should mean that you are less likely to make mistakes which can be costly and damaging. Also having the centralised support of a franchisor ensures that as issues arise you can get experienced advice and guidance to help tackle them.

I believe that franchising can be an excellent way for people, especially women, to own and run a business however as with all things in life there are pitfalls to be avoided. This book has been written to provide women considering buying a franchise with the knowledge required to make an informed decision as to which franchise to buy. This knowledge is both technically and emotionally. You need to understand what is involved in buying and running a franchise however you also need to look at yourself to identify what type of franchise you would be best suited to.

If you do decide to buy a franchise please make sure you do plenty of research to ensure the one you buy is best suited to you, and I wish you ever success.

Clive Sawyer
Managing Director, Business Options
Founder & Director, Encouraging Women into Franchising
(EWIF)

PART 1

BUYING A FRANCHISE

by Clive Sawyer

CHAPTER 1

What is franchising?

For anyone considering buying a franchise, a crucial first step is to understand what is meant by the word franchising. When people talk about buying a franchise what they are normally referring to is what is called a "Full Business Format Franchise".

The British Franchise Association (bfa) defines franchising as: "... the granting of a licence by one person (the franchisor) to another (the franchisee), which entitles the franchisee to trade under the trade mark/trade name of the franchisor and to make use of an entire package, comprising all the elements necessary to establish a previously untrained person in the business and to run it with continual assistance on a predetermined basis."

The International Franchise Association (IFA) defines franchising as:

" ... A franchise is the agreement or license between two legally independent parties which gives a person or group of people (franchisee) the right to market a product or service using the trademark or trade name of another business (franchisor). The franchisee has the right to market a product or service using the operating methods of the franchisor. The franchisee has an obligation to pay the franchisor fees for these rights whilst the franchisor has the obligation to provide rights and support to franchisees."

There are many similarities between these two definitions, most noticeably: the right to operate a business under the brand name (trade mark/trade name) of a tried and tested business. Franchising however, is much more than just operating a business using another businesses name. When buying a franchise you should get a complete package which includes all the know-how, expertise, systems and processes, training, support, and ongoing product development, that is required to run a successful profitable business.

In many countries there is specific legislation covering the sale of franchises, however in the UK, franchising is governed by standard commercial law; this means that the onus is on the franchisee to do their own due diligence. Therefore, it is important for anyone considering buying a franchise to be clear about what they are actually buying and what the legal obligations will be for them. It is also essential to understand what the franchisors obligations will be.

This book has been written as a guide specifically for women looking to buy a franchise, to help them decide what type of franchise would be right for them, how to find the right franchise and what the process is when buying a franchise.

Although specifically written with women in mind this book is equally as relevant for men or couples looking to buy a franchise.

Already in this book a number of terms which are specific to franchising have been used and therefore before going any further it is important that you are clear what these terms mean. The two main terms used to describe each party in a franchise relationship are:

The Franchisor: *This is the Head Office company that operates the franchise and sells their franchise opportunities*

The Franchisee: *This is the person who buys a franchise*

As you go through this book, there will be other franchising words used and these have been explained in the "Glossary of Terms" at the back of the book.

What is Franchising?

In simple terms, the franchisor grants a franchisee the right to operate a business using the franchisors name, branding, systems and processes, and their products and/or services, that the franchisor has successfully and profitably operated themselves.

In addition to granting rights to the franchisee, the franchisor also has an obligation to:

- continually develop the products and services that the franchisee sells, ensuring that they remain current and competitive in the marketplace.
- provide ongoing support and guidance to the franchisee.

In return for granting these rights and delivering on their obligations the franchisor will require the franchisee to pay an initial upfront fee and then ongoing monthly fees for the duration of the franchise.

When one thinks of a Full Business Format Franchise, probably the best example is McDonalds. McDonalds is the epitome of Full Business Format franchising. Wherever you go in the world you can be confident about what a Big Mac will taste like, how you will be served and the total McDonalds experience.

The History of Franchising

The term franchising can be traced back as far as the Middle Ages and was originally used to describe the granting of rights, usually by the monarch, to another individual to develop and govern over an area of land which belonged to the state. The franchisee was normally free to develop the land however they wished. In 1451, the term franchising was extended by Henry VI to mean the granting the right (franchise) to allow craftsmen to carry out their business in the City of London.

In the early nineteenth century franchising was used to define the act of voting local members of parliament. This process of voting in members of parliament was a widely abused and corrupt system. There are instances where Boroughs consisting of less than ten people where able to vote in Members of Parliament. These Boroughs became known as "rotten boroughs". The most notorious example of a rotten borough was "Old Sarum", which was a motley collection of fields rather than a community. Nonetheless, its seven voters returned two Members of Parliament! The "Great Reform Act" of 1830 saw an end to the fifty six rotten boroughs, the redistribution of some seats to the new cities and a slight reduction in the qualifications on voting. In 1832 The "Reform Act" was introduced in the boroughs giving the franchise (vote) to those who paid more than £10 a year in rates or rent.

We then move forward fifty years to 1889 when Emmeline (Emily) Pankhurst created the "Women's Franchise League", with her husband, to campaign for the right for women to vote. In 1918 Emily Pankhurst was instrumental in getting some women the right to vote. Ten years later, the "Equal Franchise Act" was passed which lowered the voting age for women to twenty one.

The term franchising was also used by the beer industry to describe when brewers allowed pubs to obtain leaseholds and sell their beer. In the nineteenth century legislation was passed to control the widespread abuse of alcohol by imposing rules on the condition of places where alcohol could be sold. This made it too costly for many individuals to own licenced premises. The rich brewers were concerned about the effect on their industry of the loss of independent pub owners. The brewers came up with a plan to circumvent the costly compliance of the new legislation for individuals by offering local pub owners the opportunity to become franchise owners. These franchisees would pay a lease on the property and working closely with the owners at a local and national level. The rich brewers would then cover the cost of complying with the legislation themselves. This is what we refer to today as the "Tied System".

In the 1970's Hollywood started using the term franchising to mean the merchandise and spin-offs related to major blockbuster films such as "Star Wars" and "James Bond" films. Franchising has also been used in connection with the rail industry. In the UK the term franchising was used in the 1993 UK Railway Act to describe offering companies the right (franchise) to operate the UK's rail network.

The first "modern" franchise in terms closely linked to the franchising (full business format franchising) that we recognise today can be traced to the US and the "Singer Sewing Machine Company". Isaac Merritt Singer invented the Singer Sewing machine in 1850. The "Singer Sewing Machine Company" in the US had developed a way of mass producing sewing machines enabling them to be sold at a price accessible to the masses. However, as more people became owners of Singer Sewing Machines throughout the US, the "Singer Sewing Machine Company" found it increasingly difficult to service these machines and offer a replacement parts service. Its solution was to establish a network of nationwide service & maintenance independent operators (franchisees).

In the 1900's "General Motors" applied the "Singer Sewing Company's" approach to the Motor industry by establishing a nationwide network of "dealers", who were granted the exclusive right (franchise) to sell and service General Motor vehicles in specific areas of the country. Throughout the middle half of the twentieth century more and more companies viewed franchising as a way of establishing both national and international coverage.

The "Wimpy" brand was created by Eddie Gold of Chicago in the 1930s. The name was inspired by the character of J. Wellington Wimpy from the Popeye cartoons created by Elzie Crisler Segar. Eddie Gold was running twelve restaurants by the early 1950s, when the concept of fast food came to the attention of the directors of J. Lyons and Co. Lyons. They decided to license the brand for use in the United Kingdom and in 1954 the first "Wimpy Bar" Lyons was established at the Lyons Corner House in Coventry Street, London. Originally the bar was a special fast-food section within the more traditional Corner House restaurants, but the success soon led to the establishment of separate Wimpy restaurants, serving only hamburger based meals. By the early 1970s the business had expanded to over a thousand restaurants in twenty three countries.

The franchising boom of the 1950s created the system, commonly known as the "Full Business Format Franchise". This acknowledged the franchise system as a distinct method of doing business rather than just having the rights to sell a product or services. The franchisee was buying a complete business package and the franchisor benefited from rapid growth with fewer resources than if they expanded through purely company owned outlets.

The popularity of franchising was affected in the 1960's as a direct result of events in both the UK and the US, which included the stock market turmoil in the US, and the fraudulent marketing scheme called pyramid selling in the UK.

The late 1970s saw the formation of the British Franchise Association (bfa) with the objective of stopping the corrupt franchise business practices, such as pyramid selling, in the UK. Within a short time the bfa earned all-party support in Parliament and its existence helped a period of rapid expansion of franchising in the UK. The founder members of the bfa include Dyno-Rod, Holiday Inns, Kentucky Fried Chicken, Prontaprint, ServiceMaster and Wimpy.

The size and reputation of the founders of the bfa brought about a level of credibility and respectability for both the bfa and franchising in the UK. This has led to the franchising sector being a major contributor to the UK economy. In 2011 the franchising sector was valued at £13.4 billion and there were 926 franchised brands, according to the NatWest annual franchise survey. The figure for the number of franchised businesses in the UK is open to dispute as there are a number of published franchise directories that show the figure as being between 1,400 and 1,600. A copy of the bfa NatWest annual franchise survey can be purchase from the bfa's bookshop at www.thebfa.org.

Types of Franchises:

There are many types of franchises available to buy in the UK. These range from your large fast food chains such as McDonald's and KFC, to your part time children's music and activity businesses such as Musical Mini's and Diddi Dance. However before you start to look at specific franchises to buy it is essential to understand the different types of franchises available and what type of franchise will meet your specific requirements.

There are three main types of franchise:

Job Franchise: This is where the franchisee typically works alone in their business or does the majority of work themselves. Examples of Job franchises would be window cleaning franchises, lawn care franchises, pet food delivery franchises, and certain training franchises.

Management Franchise: This is where the franchisee employs staff and also works on the business themselves. Examples of Management franchises would be fast food franchises, recruitment franchises and most retail outlet related franchises.

Investment Franchise: This is where the franchisee employs staff to run their franchise for them and does not take an active day to day involvement in it. Most management franchises can be run as investment franchises with the franchisee employing staff to manage and run the franchise on their behalf.

When deciding which franchise to buy it is important to understand what type of franchise suits you. There are a number of questions you should ask yourself: Do you want to work alone or with other people? Do you want to actively be involved in the business or do you want to employ a management team to run it for you? Your decision will be dependent on a number of factors including: what level of involvement you would like, your level of skill, and amount of time you can give to a business.

Having decided the type of franchise that suits your requirements you will then need to choose the sector you would like your franchise to be in. Business sectors can typically be split into 2 groups: Retail or Service industry. In its simplest terms this means whether your business will sell products or provide services. A retail business can either involve store premise where customers will visit or be an online business selling products. A service business would include businesses such as training companies or consultancy related businesses.

Next you need to decide the level of time you want to commit to your franchise. There are a large number of part time and full time franchise opportunities, with a wide range of time commitments. It is important to remember that even if a franchise says it is a Part Time business there is likely to be additional work outside the normal opening or trading hours. This typically will include franchisee administration, marketing, business planning and franchisee reporting to the franchisor.

The final consideration, when deciding what franchises to buy, is the industry sector you wish to be involved in. I believe that if you are going to have your franchise for anywhere between 5 and 15 years it is important that you like the sector your business operates in. If you don't like children then my strong advice would be not to buy a children based franchised business! If however, you like food then you may chose to look at food related franchises.

Before you start to look at any specific franchise opportunities you should spend time deciding what type of franchise will be suited to your individual needs, based on how much money you can spend, how much money you need to make, how much time you can commit to the business, how involved you want to be involved in the daily running of the business and crucially what you like to do.

CHAPTER 2

What do you get when you buy a franchise?

A Proven Model

One of the main reasons people buy a franchise rather than setting up a business from scratch is that they are buying into a profitable proven business. This means that the franchisee will benefit from all the experience, knowledge and know-how of the franchisor and can follow a model that the franchisor has refined and ironed out most of the issues.

The degree a franchise model is proven will vary between franchises. If you are looking at buying a McDonalds franchisee, which has over 1,200 stores in the UK and over 34,000 stores worldwide, you are buying a highly refined and structured business with proven profitable successful operating systems and processes. A McDonald's franchisee can be confident that if they follow the McDonalds systems then there is a very high probability that they will make the financial returns that McDonalds have stated. However, not every franchise has the kind of highly proven model that McDonalds can show. This doesn't mean that other franchises are very risky; rather it means that the level that a franchise has been proven is less. Typically the more proven a franchise, the higher the price.

As a rule, businesses should not be franchised if they haven't been trading successfully for at least two years. A franchisee needs to have confidence that they can replicate the success of the franchisor. Unfortunately in the UK there is currently no franchise law; all franchises are just covered under general commercial law. This means that there is nothing to stop any company from offering a franchise regardless how long they have been trading and also how successful they are. In fact there are a number of failing businesses that offer franchises. There are also a number of businesses that have operated for only a very short time and therefore do not have a proven business model. The UK law says that as long as the franchisor does not give misleading or untrue information to a prospective franchisee then it is the prospective franchisees responsibility to do whatever checks they feel are necessary before purchasing a franchise.

The golden rule when buying any franchise is to check that the franchisee projections provided by the franchisor are realistic and achievable. The best way to validate this is to speak to existing franchisees within the franchisors network. If the franchisor is just starting out and has no franchisees then the risk to a prospective franchisee is very high, except in the case where the franchisor has be operating themselves for a long time and their operating systems and business model are easily transferable in other parts of the country.

Everything needed to operate the franchise

When buying a franchise, typically there are three things a franchisee gets:

- The right to operate a business under the franchisors brand
- Training in how to set-up and run the franchise
- The Set-Up Package

1) The right to operate a business under the franchisors brand

Clearly when buying a franchise one expects to operate under the franchisor's particular brand using their name, logo and branding. A key benefit of buying a franchise is the brand recognition and value this brings compared with operating a business under an unknown name. Reverting to McDonalds again, when a franchisee opens a McDonald's store the majority of customers will visit it because of the McDonalds name. If one opened a burger business under an unknown brand name, it would be much harder to get the same volume of customers as a new McDonald's store. This is not a question of quality of product, rather the strength and power of brand recognition.

In 2011 there were 927 franchises in the UK and less than 10% of these would be recognisable national brands. This means that the majority of franchises in the UK do not have the benefit of brand recognition and existing high customer loyalty. These franchised businesses are not necessary risky ventures; it just means that it will take longer for franchisees to establish their businesses compared with a well known brand. The benefit of taking a lesser known franchise however is that the cost of buying the franchise will normally be much lower.

2) Training in how to set-up and run the franchise

An essential component of any franchise is the training a franchisee will receive. In all cases franchisees will be expected to follow the franchisors systems and processes exactly and therefore a franchisee must receive adequate training to allow them to do this.

This raises the question as to how much flexibility a franchisor will allow in the operation of their systems and processes. Normally franchisors allow virtually no flexibility; this is fully understandable and essential for the protection of the franchisors brand and the franchisees in the franchise network. Any franchisor that is going to allow franchisees to trade under the name has to protect the reputation of their business against bad franchisees damaging their business. The best way to protect against this is to ensure that all franchisees operate in the same way and to the exact requirements of the franchisor. If everyone operates the way the franchisor wants it is less likely that anyone can do anything that will damage the franchisors business. Similarly, franchisees should also demand and expect a franchisor to insist that all franchisees operate the same way as the value of the franchisees business will also be reduced if a franchisee damages the franchise brand. An individual franchisee can ensure that they personally do not do anything to damage the value of their business but they can not control the actions of the other franchisees in their network. Therefore they are reliant on the franchisor to monitor and ensure compliance throughout their franchise network.

Another common feature of franchising is that franchisees often have little or no industry knowledge or experience in the franchise they are buying, and there are very specific reasons for this. If you franchise a printing business it would be normal to have franchisees with no previous printing experience allowing the franchisor to train their franchisees to print their way. If franchisees have no previous printing experience then the only way they can print is the way the franchisor trains them. If however, franchisees are experienced printers then there is a high likelihood that the franchisees will print using their prior experience and previous operating methods and this may not be the way the franchisor operates. This feature of requiring no previous experience makes franchising an attractive proposition as it allows people to own and operate business in virtually any industry or business sector, regardless of experience.

The final consideration with regards training is that the training provided by the franchisor should not just be on how to operate the franchised systems but also how to sell and deliver the products and services sold. The franchisee training should also include the basics of running any business. This includes understanding the financial aspects of the business, the laws and rules of operating a business, and business planning. Many franchisees will never have run a business before and consequently may have no experience or skills in these specific areas. However, these are essential parts of running any business and it is unrealistic to expect to run any successful business without having these skills. It is therefore important that the training provided by the franchisor covers all these areas and fully prepares the franchisee for running their business.

3) The Set-Up Package

In the UK most franchises are what are known as "turn-key" businesses. This means the franchisor will provide the franchisee with everything required to set-up and launch their business.

In McDonalds case, McDonalds will co-ordinate the total fit-out of their franchisees store; have the initial stock delivered; provide store menus and all in-store signage, provide a comprehensive operations manual covering all aspects of running a McDonalds store; give the franchisee all the forms and contracts they will require to recruit staff; provide training for the franchisee and their staff; co-ordinate a marketing launch campaign with the store; and provide an area manager to support the franchisee in the development and launch of their franchise whilst providing ongoing support and guidance. In essence everything a franchisee will need to launch and run a successful McDonalds business.

When looking at which franchise to buy it is important to be absolutely clear what the franchisor will provide within their Set-Up Package and what the franchisee is expected to source and fund themselves.

In an attempt to keep the published cost of a franchise down, some franchisors exclude certain items required by a franchisee to launch their business. This will not only increase the overall cost of the franchise but if the franchisee is left to their own devices to identify and source additional elements required for the business, compromise the franchisees business. It has already been highlighted that many franchisees have little or no skills in the franchise sector they are purchasing and therefore to expect an inexperienced franchisee to identify and source elements required for their business will inevitably lead to mistakes, sometimes costly, being made.

Where a "turn-key" franchise is not offered, it is important to identify what is left for the franchisee to source and fund themselves, how much this will cost, and what guidance the franchisor will provide to ensure the franchisee sources the right items.

Ongoing Support

When buying a franchise, it should not be viewed as a one-off transaction. By this I mean that the franchisor's obligations to the franchisee do not stop once the franchisee launches their business.

Clearly the franchisor has an essential role in assisting the franchisee to set-up and launch their business. Equally important however is the ongoing support the franchisee receives from the franchisor. This support ongoing typically covers 4 areas:

- Support in running a successful business
- Operational compliance
- Research and Development
- Centrally provided services

1) Support in running a successful business

The franchisor should provide regular support to help their franchisees run a successful and profitable business. Often the support is delivered to franchisees through a network of Area Managers who will regularly visit franchisees and who are also available remotely for day to day advice and guidance.

Area Managers typically help franchisees to assess the performance of their business, identify areas for improvements, suggest ways to improve marketing, and ultimately help to grow the franchisees business.

Often an area of weakness for many franchisees relates to financial management. For any business to have sustainable success, it is imperative that the business owner fully understands the financial state of their business and is aware of the financial implications on their business of any action they take, whether that relates to recruiting more staff, changing suppliers, undertaking marketing or just managing their business to suit the economic climate.

Mathematics, numbers, and financial analysis are often things that people love or hate. If you love numbers and financial analysis then you will be half way to running a successful business as the ultimate success of a business relates to finance and profitability. However if the thought of numbers and financial analysis makes you cringe then you might need assistance and support in this specific area. Area Managers should be there to help franchisees analyse the performance of the franchisees business against key ratio's and statistics. They will be able to identify how a franchise is performing and what areas of the business the franchisee may need to focus on to improve the success and profitability of the business. If the franchisors Area Managers do not provide this service, the franchisee will need to either recruit someone with the necessary skills or find outsourced financial support.

Area Managers should also provide advice and guidance on all operational questions and issues that a franchisee may have. This could relate to issues such as staffing, sales techniques, service delivery, and anything involved in the day to day running of the business. Area Managers will be able to explain the standard operating procedures a franchisee is required to follow whilst also providing best practice from the whole franchisee network. Franchisees should view their Area Manager as a fundamental part of their own management team.

2) Operational compliance

Operational compliance means how a franchisee follows and implements the franchisors systems and processes. As has been previously stated, operational compliance is essential in every franchise, from the franchisors, franchisees and customers perspective.

The franchisor must ensure that any person who operates under their brand name does not do anything to damage the reputation of their business. When franchising, a franchisor will have many franchisees spread across the country all operating under their brand name. This could potentially be a recipe for disaster for a franchisor and therefore the best way of protecting the reputation of the franchisors business is to ensure that every franchisee operates exactly the same and in exact accordance to the proven systems and process of the franchisor. It is for this precise reason that franchisees are trained in the exact methods of the franchisor and are provided with a highly detailed Franchise Operations Manual which states exactly how a franchisee should carry out every aspect of their business.

From a franchisees perspective, one should expect to see a highly structured operating system supported by detailed Operating Manuals, this will not just help a franchisee follow the franchisors proven business model but also helps to protect the franchisees investment.

When one buys a franchise, one of the essential components that makes the business model a franchise rather than any other expansion model is that the franchisee owns their business and they have the right to sell it. Therefore part of the value of buying a franchise is the future value of the business when a franchisee comes to sell. Therefore a franchisee will not want anything to happen to affect the value of their franchise business.

An element of protecting the value of a franchise is in the franchisees own hands. So long as the franchisee runs a profitable business there will be people who will want to buy the franchise from them. However, there is one area where the franchisee has no control over the impact on the value of their business and that is the performance of the other franchisees in the network. If another franchisee does something to damage the overall brand then they are not just damaging it for themselves but also every other franchisee in their network. Therefore franchisees should want to see highly structured systems and processes supported by detailed Operating Manuals to control the way all franchisees operate. Franchisees should also want to see that the franchisor has a process for ensuring franchisee compliance. This is normally achieved through franchisees having to send in regular reports and checklists, and through Area Manager visits to audit compliance. Having highly structured systems and process with compliance audits should be something a franchisee should insist on.

3) Research and Development

Most franchises are granted for five years with an option to renew for one, two or more additional five year terms. This means that a franchisee could have the business for ten or fifteen years; this is a long time in any business and it is essential that the customer offering is continually developed to ensure that it remains current and competitive in the marketplace. You just need to look back 15 years to see how the business environment has changed and the impact technology and new products have had on all businesses.

It would be impractical to expect franchisees to research and develop new products or services as it is unlikely that a franchisee would have the necessary skills or experience to develop new products or services. In addition a franchisor will not want their franchisees introducing their own new ideas within their own businesses as franchisors need to maintain consistency of product offering across the whole franchise network. Therefore the responsibility for research and development must therefore lie with the franchisor.

Ideally the franchisor will undertake research and development and then trial and evaluate new products or services, normally with their Head Office staff or through Head Office outlets. Only once the franchisor is confident that the new product or service will work will they roll it out across their franchise network. From the franchisees perspective this means that they will continually have new products and services to keep their business competitive and current.

4) Centrally Provided Services

Many franchises are structured so that the franchisor provides a range of centrally delivered services on behalf of their franchisees. These services range from handling customer enquiries, issuing invoices, bookkeeping, and undertaking national marketing on behalf of the franchisee. These centrally provided services will vary between franchises; however, centrally provided services have the benefit of utilising the franchisors skills and technical experience for the benefit of all franchisees, achieving economies of scale and consistency through central coordination and delivery of services, and freeing up the franchisee to concentrate on income generation activities.

When looking at different franchises it is important to be very clear what parts of the business will be provided centrally by the franchisor and what will be the responsibility of the franchisee. It is important to be aware that the more a franchisee is expected to do themselves, typically the more resources the franchisee will need which in turn will increase their overall operating costs, reducing their profitability.

Franchise Resales

When buying a new franchise, the one thing not normally included are existing customers. With most franchises you will be required to launch your franchise business from scratch and build your own customer base with the support of your franchisor.

A key component of a franchise however, is that the franchisee owns their business and has the right to sell it. There are many reasons why franchisees look to sell their businesses, ranging from ill health, retirement, wanting a new challenge or just wanting to realise the value they have built up in their business.

In the UK there is an established franchise resale market, which allows people looking to buy a franchise, the opportunity to buy a franchise business that is established, has a track record and an existing customer base. Buying an existing franchise business can offer many advantages as it allows a franchisee to start trading at an optimum level immediately, takes away some of the risks of establishing a business, and reduces the lead time between signing the Franchise Agreement and starting trading. Not surprisingly these benefits come at a cost, which is that franchise resales are usually substantially more expensive than buying a new franchise direct from the franchisor. Often this extra cost is well justified and the benefits outweigh the additional cost however, some franchisees look to sell at inflated prices, in which case a franchisee may be better off buying a new franchise direct from the franchisor.

When deciding whether to buy a franchise, part of the decision making process should include whether you would be better to buy a new franchise and launch your franchise business yourself or pay extra to buy an existing franchise that is already trading.

CHAPTER 3

Where to find suitable franchises

If you have decided that franchising is for you, you need to know where to look to be able to find a selection of suitable franchises to choose from. There are two different marketing sectors to look at: 1) Specialist Franchise Media 2) Non Franchise Media.

Within each different sector, Franchise and Non Franchise media, there are a wide range of places to look and these are often broken down into 5 distinct areas: 1) Online Media   2) Printed Media 3) Exhibitions 4) Word of Mouth 5) Franchise Broker

Specialist Franchise Media

Probably the most obvious place to start looking for suitable franchises to buy is in specialist franchise media. Given the size of the franchise industry and number of franchises that exist, it is not surprising that there are many different places that franchise opportunities are advertised.

1) Online Media:

There are a large number of websites that advertise franchises opportunities. The first and most obvious place to look is on a franchisors own website. Virtually all franchisors will have a page on their website that provides basic information about their franchise opportunity and how to register an interest in their franchise.

There are also a large number of dedicated franchise websites that advertise a wide range of franchises for sale. These websites normally list franchises under various industry categories. Each franchise within a category normally has a dedicated page that lists details about the franchise, typically what the franchise business does, how much it will cost and what is included in the franchise price. There are a large number of dedicated franchise advertising websites, and the main ones are listed in the "Sources of Help" section at the back of this book.

An important website to look at is the British Franchise Association's, www.thebfa.org. The British Franchise Association (bfa) is the only recognised Franchise Association in the UK. The bfa was established in 1978 with the aim of regulating franchising on an ethical basis, by granting membership to those franchisors that it considers meets the demands of its Codes of Ethics and procedures.

The bfa operates a membership system for franchised businesses that meet its standards and these are split into three categories: Full, Associate and Provisional. Membership of any of the three categories is through a formal accreditation process which ensures the Franchise Model being offered is a realistic refection of what franchisees can expect to achieve, that the Franchise Agreement is fair, and that the overall franchise meets the European Code of Ethics in Franchising.

However, purchasing a bfa member franchise is no guarantee of success; what it does ensure however is that the franchise meets industry standards and that the projections provided by the franchisor are realistic. To be a successful franchisee will still require a lot of hard work and dedication however this is true of owning and running any business.

The bfa's website www.thebfa.org has a list of all its members split by the three categories and against each franchise there will be an overview of the franchise being offered and a facility to request further information from the franchisor.

2) Printed Media

There are a number of different types of printed media that advertises franchise opportunities. These can be split into three groups: 1) Franchise Magazines 2) Franchise Directories 3) National Newspapers

Franchise Magazines:

In the UK there are four dedicated franchise magazines and

one magazine that is half franchising and half other business opportunities. A list of these magazines can be found in the "Sources of Help" section at the back of this book.

All of these magazines carry a combination of general articles about franchising, advertisements for franchises, and a general listing of franchise opportunities. When thinking of buying any franchise it is important to do your research and the franchise articles in these magazines are a good source of general information.

When looking at the franchise advertisements it is important not to get carried away by the big double page colour advertisements; just because an advertisement is large and glossy has no bearing on whether the franchise is good or not. Unlike the British Franchise Association's accreditation process, most of the magazines do not check the standard and validity of the franchises they advertise. Franchising in the UK is only covered by general commercial law, which states that it is up to the individual buying a franchise to have performed their own due diligence; it is up to you to do a full check of the franchise before signing any Agreement or parting with any money. In the next chapter we will look at the material checks any prospective franchisee should make before buying a franchise.

Franchise Directories:

There are two specialist Franchise Directories which lists virtually all the franchise opportunities in the UK. A list of these Franchise Directories can be found in the "Sources of Help" section at the back of this book.

These directories are a good resource to show the wide range of sectors offering franchise opportunities and all the main franchises you can buy in each. It is important to know that in their bid to be the Franchise Directory with the most listings, both Franchise Directories contain the names of old franchises that are no longer franchising or worse still have gone out of business. Having said this both Franchise Directories can help prospective franchisees narrow down the type of franchise they are interested in and the various franchises on offer.

National Newspapers:

Virtually all the main national newspapers carry a feature on franchising at least once a week. The features are normally a combination of an article on a specific sector in franchising and a number of advertisements for franchises. A list of the national newspapers that cover franchising can be found in the "Sources of Help" section at the back of this book.

As with the Franchise Magazines, most of the national newspapers do not carry out much if any checks as to the validity or claims of the franchises being advertised. However, the articles and features are yet another source of information which can help improve the knowledge of any prospective franchisee before they buy a franchise.

3) Exhibitions:

Exhibitions provide prospective franchisees with a good opportunity to see a variety of franchisees all in one place and talk to franchisors in person. The Franchise Exhibitions in the UK can be split into two categories 1) National Exhibitions 2) Local Exhibitions. A list of Franchise Exhibition Organisers can be found in the "Sources of Help" section at the back of this book.

National Franchise Exhibitions:

All the National Franchise Exhibitions in the UK are run by just two Franchise Exhibition Organisers. The main difference between the Franchise Exhibitions run by these Exhibition Organisers is that in those run by Venture Marketing Group require all exhibiting franchises to be either British Franchise Association (bfa) accredited members or have undergone a lesser exhibition status check by the bfa. The Franchise Exhibitions run by Prysm MFV do not make this a requirement and therefore you will see bfa accredited and non bfa accredited franchises on sale. At this point it is worth stating that in 2011 less than 1/3rd of all franchises in the UK were bfa members.

National Franchise Exhibitions in the UK are normally run at the beginning of the year, February and March, and also in the autumn in September and October. Depending on the popularity of the Exhibition, a prospective franchisee could expect to see between 60 and 140 different franchise exhibitors. These National Franchise Exhibitions also run a large number of seminars explaining all aspects of franchising as well as having industry specialists on hand to give advice.

Local Franchise Exhibitions:

There are a number of local Franchise Exhibitions run in large towns and cities across the UK. As their name implies they typically have a very local slant, with only franchisors that are looking to recruit franchisees in that specific geographic area exhibiting. This means that the number of franchises exhibiting at these local Franchise Exhibitions is much smaller than the national Franchise Exhibitions. The benefit as an attendee at one of these local Franchise Exhibitions is that you will know that the franchises on show will have franchise opportunities available in the local area.

4) Word of Mouth:

This may seem a strange category to include as a way to find a franchise, however in 2011 there were over 36,000 franchisees in the UK with 89% being satisfied or fully satisfied, according to the NatWest Annual Franchise Survey 2012. This means that there are tens of thousands of contented franchisees who are happy to promote the benefits of their franchise.

As a prospective franchisee, I would give more credibility to the testimonials of an existing franchisee that has parted with money and is actually running a franchise, than the words of a franchisor that may just be concerned in selling franchises. Regardless as to whether you hear about a franchise opportunity from an existing franchisee or not, it is always sensible to speak to existing franchisees of the franchise you are considering buying to get their first hand experience BEFORE you buy.

5) Franchise Brokers:

The final way of finding a franchise is by utilising the services of a specialist Franchise Broker. There are a number of companies that offer to help prospective franchisees identify which type of franchise they would be suited to and provide a list of franchisees that meet their requirements.

These Franchise Broker companies can provide valuable assistance in enabling a prospective franchisee decide the type of franchise they would be suited to and what suitable franchises exist. The majority of these Franchise Brokers also do not charge a prospective franchisee for their service. So what is the catch?

There isn't necessary a catch, however it is important to

understand how these Franchise Brokers make their money. The majority of Franchise Brokers make their money from charging the franchisor a commission for finding them suitable franchisees; therefore in effect they are working for the franchisor not the franchisee. This means that they will only offer and promote franchise opportunities where the franchisor will pay them. There may also be a conflict of interest even amongst the franchises they promote, as different franchisors will pay them differing levels of commission, which means there is the potential conflict between recommending the most suitable franchises and those that provide them with the highest commission from.

So long as you are happy to do your own research as to what other franchise opportunities exist outside those offered by a Franchise Broker, using the services of a Franchise Broker can be helpful in identifying suitable franchises. For a truly independent service I would recommend you look for a Franchise Broker that charges prospective franchisees direct. Whilst this will cost you money, it is a good investment given that you will be making one of the most important decisions of your life when you buy a franchise. It makes good sense to pay for a truly independent service which can recommend any franchise rather than just the franchises that will pay them a commission.

Non Franchise Media

It may seem strange to suggest that you look for franchise opportunities to buy in non franchise media however there are many non franchise media sites and publications that advertise franchises for sale. These non franchise media are normally either: 1) Trade 2) Consumer or 3) Lifestyle Media.

Within each different Non Franchise media sector, there are a wide range of places to look and these are often broken down into 3 distinct areas: 1) Online Media   2) Printed Media   3) Exhibitions

1) Trade Media:

Many trade sectors will have websites and publications dedicated to their industry. In the construction industry for instance there are publications such as Construction News. In the food industry there are publications and websites such as The Grocer or The Publican. Often you will find franchises specific to the individual industry advertised within these industry specific publications, websites and exhibitions.

The Armed Forces and Police Force also have trade publications which advertise franchise opportunities as many franchisors see the discipline and background of Armed Forces and Police personnel well suited to franchising.

2) Consumer Media:

Before franchisors decide to advertise their franchise opportunities they will have profiled the type of people suited to become one of their franchisees. Once they have created a franchisee profile they will then specifically advertise in media that targets the profile of people they are looking for.

Some part time franchises are well suited to women with children and provide a second income opportunity that can work around the demands of raising a family. Consequently franchisors will often advertise in consumer media that targets this group such as supermarket magazines and parenting publications.

Some franchisors actively target more mature people as their franchisees. In these cases they may advertise in media focused at an older age group such as on Saga's website or in the Saga magazine as the only people who typically look at their publications will be over the age of 50.

3) Lifestyle Media:

There are also a range of media that specifically targets the hobbies and lifestyle of individuals. Franchises that are activity based such as sports related franchises may choose to advertise is sport related media. Therefore if you are looking to buy a Health and Fitness franchise, it would be worth looking for franchise opportunities in publications such as Health & Fitness Magazine or on websites such as www.womensfitnesss.co.uk. There are also a wide range of media targeting gay and lesbians which also advertise specific franchise opportunities.

In summary, franchise opportunities are advertised in a wide and diverse range of media which include both specialist franchise and non franchise media. When you have identified the type of franchise that suits you, check both franchise and non franchise media for suitable franchise opportunities.

CHAPTER 4

Buying a franchise: the process

The process for buying any franchise is relatively similar. In this chapter we will look at the standard franchise recruitment process from requesting information on a franchise, registering an interest in a franchise, to having an interview with a franchisor, reviewing the Franchise Agreement, and finally signing the Franchise Agreement and becoming a franchisee.

At every step of the franchise recruitment process it is important to remember that the onus is on you to do your own due diligence to check that the information you are provided with is accurate and ultimately that the franchise is suitable for you and your needs. The franchisor is not allowed to falsify information or deliberately misinform you however there are many ways to portray information which would not strictly be lying but may be a creative way of imparting information. For this we only have to look at the way estate agents used to market their smallest property as being low maintenance, compact and bijou! Immediate apologies to any estate agent that might find this light hearted illustration offensive!

When buying a franchise there are typically 7 steps:

- Getting basic information on a franchise
- Registering an interest in a franchise
- An interview with the franchisor
- Assessing the suitability of a franchise
- The franchise offer
- Understanding the Franchise Agreement
- Signing the Franchise Agreement

1) Getting basic information on a franchise:

When you have decided what type of franchise suits you, and what franchise opportunities exist that meet your requirements, the first step is to request initial information on the franchise opportunity. All franchisors should have a document that is a high level summary of their franchise opportunity, which is called either the "Franchise Brochure" or "Franchise Prospectus"; both terms mean the same thing.

The "Franchise Brochure" should provide you with a minimum 6 things:

What the franchise business does

The name of a franchisee does not necessary give any indication as to what the business does. If one didn't know what Virgin did, you wouldn't be able to guess from the name that they were music publishers, a multimedia broadcaster, and a national train operator. Therefore, the "Franchise Brochure" should say what the business does, for example "Recognition Express" franchises sell promotional items and franchisees of "Oscars" sell and deliver pet food.

How much the franchise costs

It is essential at the earliest stage you know what the total cost of the franchise might be. If you can not afford it then there is no point spending any more time considering that particular franchise opportunity.

When the "Franchise Brochure" states the cost of the franchise, make sure you know what is included in the cost. Good franchises will state the Total Investment required for the franchise. The Total Investment will include the cost of buying the franchise, the cost of setting up and launching the business, and also the working capital a franchisee will require. However as there is no legislation in the UK to stipulate what a franchisor should include in their published price, unlike the US and Australia, less scrupulous franchisors will exclude certain costs in an attempt to keep the published price low and therefore make it potentially more attractive to prospective franchisees.

Franchise Profit and Loss projections

This is an essential piece of information required at the outset for any prospective franchisee because if the profitability projections do not meet your requirements then there is no point spending any more time considering that particular franchise. As with the published cost of the franchise it is essential you are clear what is included within the Profit & Loss projections and also on what basis they have been calculated.

It is very important to know whether the franchisee will be expected to work in the business and be expected to carry out certain roles. If this is the case then you must know whether the Profit & Loss projections include a salary for the franchisee or whether the franchisee is expected to be remunerated out of the profits of the business.

It is also important to understand the basis on which the Profit & Loss projections have been calculated; if the figures quoted are based on the actual average performance of franchisees in the network, the actual performance of the franchisor, or projections which have no basis of proven evidence. If the projections are based on actual franchisee performance it is important to know if the projections are those achieved by the best franchisees, worst franchisees or an average of the franchisee network. It is also important to remember that there is no guarantee of profitability in franchising and therefore understanding the basis of the Profit & Loss projections shown in the "Franchise Brochure" is only an indication as to how realistic they will be to achieve.

The franchisee role

As was explained in the first chapter of this book there are many different types of franchise and therefore it is important that the "Franchise Brochure" clearly explains what type of franchise is being marketed. Is the franchise an "Investment", "Management" or "Job" franchise? Is the franchise part-time or full-time? Will you be required to manage staff or is it a single person business? If it is a service business will you be carrying out a service, such as cleaning windows in a window cleaning franchise, driving a van in a pet food delivery franchise, or teaching people to sing in a choir franchise? If it is a franchise selling products will you be the one doing to the selling and if so does this involve knocking on people's doors, cold calling on the telephone or following up customer enquiries. The role the franchisee will be expected to take in their franchise will be a major factor in whether you will be suited to the franchise.

Whether the franchise has been independently assessed

If the franchise is a member of the British Franchise Association (bfa) or has been reviewed and pre-approved for funding by one of the High Street Franchise Banks it should tell you. The contact details of the bfa and the High Street Franchise Banks can be found in the "Sources of Help" section at the back of this book.

Although buying an independently assessed franchise is no

guarantee of success, it does mean however that the way the franchise has been set up, the basis of the Profit & Loss projections and the fairness of the Franchise Agreement, are a true reflection of the actual franchise and meet the European Code of Ethics for franchising.

What to do next if you are still interested
The "Franchise Brochure" should explain the next steps a person should follow if they are still interested in the franchise opportunity.

Some "Franchise Brochures" will contain additional information about the franchise opportunity, however, the six components listed above are absolutely essential information to enable a person to decide whether the franchise is suited to them and whether to move to the next stage in the franchise recruitment process.

2) Registering an interest in the franchise:
Having reviewed the "Franchise Brochure" and decided that it does potentially meet your requirements, the next step in the recruitment process is registering your interest in the franchise opportunity. This normally takes the form of informing the franchisor and completing a "Franchise Application Form".

Informing the franchisor of your interest can be as simple as completing a form on the franchisors website or emailing the franchisor expressing your interest. The franchisor should then send you their "Franchise Application Form" to complete.

It is important to know that by completing and submitting a "Franchise Application Form" you are not committing to anything. You are totally free to pull out or change your mind with no repercussions.

"Franchise Application Forms" vary greatly but typically are split into 3 sections:

Personal information

The franchisor will want to have some basic information about who is interested in their franchise. This should typically include the individual's name, contact details and educational background. It is perfectly reasonable for a franchisee to request these details and the franchisor is only allowed under data protection legislation to use them in their process of evaluating a person's suitability as a franchisee.

Financial status

The franchisor will expect you to tell them how much money you have and whether you will require financial assistance/ bank loan in order to buy their franchise. The franchisor will want to know that you have sufficient money to buy the franchise or are likely to be able to raise the balance of funds required. If you haven't sufficient money or can't raise the money then the franchisor will not want to waste time pursuing your application.

Relevant experience

Most "Franchise Application Forms" will also ask the applicant to provide examples of their experience in areas which are relevant to the franchise. If the franchise involves selling, the franchisor may ask the applicant to provide some background on their sales experience. If the franchise involves a high level of numeracy such as a bookkeeping franchise then the franchisor will rightly want to know whether the applicant is numerate and have any financial or bookkeeping experience.

The franchise recruitment process is a two way process. You will be assessing the suitability of the franchise and the franchisor will be assessing your suitability as a prospective franchisee; therefore be prepared to provide the franchisor with basic information at this point in the process.

3) An interview for the franchisor:

On receiving a "Franchise Application Form" a franchisor will assess whether they think the applicant meets the basic criteria they are looking for in their franchisees. For those suitable "Franchise Application Forms", the franchisor will invite the applicant to a "Franchise Interview". The "Franchise Interview" is an opportunity for the applicant to find out far more detailed information about the franchise. The "Franchise Interview" is also an opportunity for the franchisor to make an assessment as to whether the applicant would be suitable as a franchisee. The "Franchise Interview" typically consists of 4 parts:

Questioning the applicant

Most franchisors start a "Franchise Interview" by asking the applicant questions about the information on the applicants "Franchise Application Form" and other relevant questions to help the franchisor assess the applicant's suitability as a prospective franchisee.

Good franchisors take the assessment of prospective franchisees very seriously as they only want to sell franchises to people they believe have a real chance of being a successful franchisee.

Detailed information about the franchise opportunity
In order that an applicant can also decide whether a franchise is suitable for them, they must be provided with all the detailed information about the franchise opportunity in order to be able to make an informed decision.

In the UK, unlike other countries, there is no legislation that states what information a franchisor should provide a prospective franchisee. Good franchisors will provide applicants with a "Franchise Disclosure Document" containing detailed information about the franchise opportunity. The franchisor should go through the "Franchise Disclosure

Document" with the applicant at the "Franchise Interview" and should permit the applicant to take the "Franchise Disclosure Document" away with them.

The "Franchise Disclosure Document" should contain detailed information about:

- What the franchisee gets when they buy the franchise
- What training a franchisee will receive
- The role of the franchisee
- What central services will be provided by the franchisor
- A breakdown of the total cost of the franchise
- What the ongoing fees will be
- Whether they will be granted an exclusive or non exclusive territory
- What basis the franchisee's territory will be created
- Whether there are any minimum performance criteria to adhere to
- How long the franchise is granted for
- What the policy is for renewing franchises
- What the policy is for selling an existing franchise
- Detailed monthly Profit & Loss and Cash Flow Projections

If the "Franchise Disclosure Document" is going to be of help in assessing the suitability of the franchise for an applicant it will contain confidential information. It is therefore entirely reasonable that the franchisor will ask applicants to sign a

"Confidentiality Agreement". The "Confidentiality Agreement" is a legal document which the applicant signs to confirm that they will not disclosure any confidential information to any third party and will only use the information to help assess whether to buy the franchise. The legal obligation not to disclose the franchisors confidential information remains in place even after an applicant decides whether or not to continue with their application to buy the franchise.

Applicants questions

The "Franchise Disclosure Document" should cover all aspects of the franchise however it is likely that the applicant will still have specific questions which may not have been covered or answered in full by the "Franchise Disclosure Document". The "Franchise Interview" should provide the applicant with an opportunity to ask any question they may still have.

It is extremely important that applicants raise any issues or question they still have and fully understand the answers that are given. The "Franchise Interview" is often the only formal meeting with a franchisor before the franchisor makes an offer to an applicant. As has previously been stated, deciding whether to buy a franchise may be one of the most important decisions you ever take and therefore making sure you fully understand what your are buying and what will be expected of you is essential. Do not let embarrassment stop you asking any questions or seeking clarification on any answer you don't fully understand. Pride often comes before a fall and a fall in franchising can be very costly!

Next steps

The last part of the "Franchise Interview" should be an explanation of what happens, after the interview. The franchisor should explain when they will indicate to the applicant whether they are prepared to offer them a franchise and if they do the process they must follow if the want to accept the offer.

Most franchisors will insist that "Franchise Interviews" take place at the franchisors Head Office premise. Applicants should also expect this as it should be part of the applicant's assessment of the franchise to see what infrastructure the franchisor has to support their franchisees. Do they have an in-house training facility; are there area managers to support franchisees; is there a research and development department; what facilities have they to support a growing franchisee network? All of these things are best checked out in person at the franchisors Head Office.

The extent of the franchisors Head Office facilities should be part of your decision as to whether to buy a franchise. Your decision should not just be based on how extensive the franchisors facilities are, rather how suitable the facilities are. Some small franchises will be operated from the franchisors house; this does not necessary mean they are inadequate in their support to their franchisees since it depends what central services and support they state they will provide to their franchisees. At the other end of the scale, just because a franchisor has an extremely impressive Head Office does not mean that they will properly support their franchisees.

4) Assessing the suitability of the franchise:

Having attended the "Franchise Interview" and been provided with detailed information about the franchise opportunity it is important to carry out your own due diligence.

Firstly you need to assess, having had the detailed information provided at the "Franchise Interview" whether the franchise still meets all your requirements. Is the cost of the franchise what you thought it was or are there additional costs that take the franchise out of your price range? Is the role of the franchisee something you are comfortable doing? How realistic are the profit projections? Is the franchisors infrastructure able to provide the support you require to run a successful business?

Next, it is important to get first hand feedback on what it is actually like to be a franchisee of the business. The easiest and best way of doing this is to speak to current franchisees. Good franchisors should be prepared to provide you with the contact details of all their franchisees and should be happy for you to speak to any one of them; however in reality often franchisors will only provide the contact details of a select few franchisees. If this is the case you need to consider whether the franchisor is just giving you the contact details of their best franchisees and not those who are either failing or are unhappy with the franchisor.

Unhappy and failing franchisees are as important to talk to as the best performing franchisees since you need to understand the reasons why they might be failing or unhappy. When speaking to less happy franchisees it is important to put their comments into context, as there will always be people in all walks of life that are negative. Just because a franchisee is unhappy or failing does not necessary mean the franchise is bad; there may be good reasons why the franchisee is unhappy and that might be down to the individual franchisee and not the franchisor. However getting all sides of the story is important BEFORE you make any final decision.

If a franchisor does not give you the contact details of every franchisee in their network there is nothing wrong with you finding the franchisees contact details yourself. Normally the franchisors website will give the details of all their franchisees. If so, just call or email them direct. If the franchisors website does not provide this information then consider Googling the franchisees or using a search directory such as Yell.com. How you get the contact details will vary however I would never advocate buying a franchise without having spoken to a number of franchisees first.

5) The Franchise offer:

Following the "Franchise Interview", the franchisor will normally either offer you a provisional offer subject to references or will inform you that they are not taking your application any further.

The franchise offer will state the conditions under which the offer is being made and the franchise territory that is being offered. The offer will also explain the steps the applicant will need to take to accept the offer. This can include: formally accepting the offer; paying a deposit in order to receive the Franchise Agreement; formal confirmation that the applicant has the necessary funds to purchase the franchise, and suitable references being received.

Where a franchisor requires an applicant to pay a deposit prior to the release of the Franchise Agreement, there are a number of things to check:

- Whether the deposit is refundable less any third party franchisor costs. This is industry best practice and a requirement of the British Franchise Association (bfa).

- Whether there is a timescale between paying the deposit and having to make a final decision and signing the Franchise Agreement. The bfa are against any franchise which puts undue pressure on an applicant to sign a Franchise Agreement including putting short time limits on an individual to make a decision.

- Whether the franchisor will continue to take additional enquiries or not for the same franchise territory being offered to you. The bfa are again against franchisors putting pressure on applicants to sign a Franchise Agreement by putting them in a race against applicants to sign for a specific franchise territory.

Franchise deposits are a very normal practice and people should not be concerned by them so long as the conditions surrounding them are reasonable.

If a franchisor turns down an applicant then there is nothing the individual can do so long as the franchisor has not made their decision based on gender, religion or sexual orientation. Buying a franchise is not like going for a job interview where the job interviewee is protected by employment legislation. A franchisor can chose who they want to sell their franchise to and does not have to give any reason for declining an applicant.

6) Understanding the Franchise Agreement:

The "Franchise Agreement", is the legal document that lays

out the conditions that the franchise is granted under and the obligations on both the franchisee and the franchisor. Most "Franchise Agreements", specifically state that the franchisee has undertaken their own due diligence before signing the "Franchise Agreement" and that the franchisee is happy to enter into the franchise on the terms contained within it. The "Franchise Agreement", also specifically states that any verbal information given to franchisee is invalid unless it is included within the "Franchise Agreement". It is therefore essential that any prospective franchisee takes specialist franchise advice to ensure they fully understand what they are being granted under the "Franchise Agreement" and what their obligations will be and those of the franchisor.

Most franchisors will not permit any changes to their "Franchise Agreement". This is quite normal practice as the franchisor wants all their franchisees to operate their franchises on the same or similar terms. This is because operationally it is much easier to deal with franchisees all in the same way and because it also adds value to the franchisors business. Treating all franchisees the same is also a demonstration of the franchisors commitment to fair treatment throughout their franchisee network. Should the franchisor ever wish to sell their franchised business, purchasers will want a standard franchise network all on the same terms.

It is important not to be alarmed or concerned about the possibility that a franchisor might sell their franchise business.

The law protects franchisees by ensuring that any purchaser of a franchise business must continue to operate the business as a franchise under the terms of the existing franchisees contract.

It is important also to seek the advice of people who are specialist in franchising to assist in fully understanding the obligations within the "Franchise Agreement". The British Franchise Association (bfa) has member solicitors who are specialists in franchising. These solicitors will offer prospective franchisees a service to review their "Franchise Agreement" and advise them whether the terms of the "Franchise Agreement" are reasonable, what their obligations will be, what the franchisors is obligated to do and whether the "Franchise Agreement" complies with both the bfa's rules and the European Code of ethics in Franchising. A list of bfa member solicitors can be found on the bfa website at www. thebfa.org.

There is a temptation for prospective franchisees to try and save money by either just reviewing the "Franchise Agreement" themselves or using a general commercial solicitor who will charge less than a specialist bfa member solicitor. As has been stated on a number of different occasions, buying a franchise will probably be one of the biggest decisions you will make in your life. Given that UK legislation states that by signing a "Franchise Agreement", you are stating that you fully understand and accept the conditions of the "Franchise Agreement", making one of your biggest decisions without specialist advice would appear to be extremely foolish.

7) Signing the Franchise Agreement:

The final step in buying a franchise is the signing of the "Franchise Agreement". Having assessed the type of franchise that would suit you, requested information on suitable franchises, met with a number of franchisors, reviewed the detailed information about those suitable franchisees, talked with existing franchisees, paid a deposit on your chosen franchise, and taken specialist franchise legal advice on the "Franchise Agreement", you are now ready to sign the "Franchise Agreement" and become a franchisee.

The signing of the "Franchise Agreement", is the formal last stage of the process of buying a franchise. You will need to sign the "Franchise Agreement", in person with the franchisor and the "Franchise Agreement", will need to be witnessed by someone who was not involved in the franchise recruitment process.

Having signed the "Franchise Agreement", and paid the balance of any franchise fees due, you are now officially a franchise and you will be entering a new exciting chapter of your life.

CHAPTER 5

Summary

What is Franchising

Franchising has been used over centuries to mean different things in different situations. In the UK when buying a franchise you will be buying what is known as a "Full Business Format Franchise". This provides franchisees with a complete proven business operating under the brand name of the franchisor and with ongoing support and guidance.

Types of Franchise

There are three main types of franchise:

Job Franchise: This is where the franchisee typically works alone in their business or does the majority of work themselves
Management Franchise: This is where the franchisee employs staff and also works on the business themselves
Investment Franchise: This is where the franchisee employs staff to run their franchise for them and does not take an active day to day involvement in it

Having decided the type of franchise that you would like and that would suit you, it is essential to consider the sector you want your franchise to be in: Retail or Service industry. Next you need to decide the level of time you can commit to your franchise: Part Time or Full Time franchise. Finally you need to consider what industry sector you want to be involved in.

What You Get When You Buy a Franchise:
When buying a franchise, typically there are three things a franchisee gets:

- The right to operate a business under the franchisors brand
- Training in how to run the franchise
- A Set-Up Package that includes everything you will require to launch your franchise business

Franchise Resales

When deciding whether to buy a franchise, part of the decision making process should include whether you should buy a new franchise and launch your franchise business yourself or pay extra to buy an existing franchise that is already trading.

Ongoing Support

The franchisor has an essential role in assisting the franchisee to set-up and launch their business. Equally important is the ongoing support the franchisee will receive from their franchisor. This support typically covers four areas:

- Support in running a successful business
- Support in how to comply with all operational requirements of the business
- Research and Development of new products and services
- Delivery of centrally provided services for the franchisee

Where to Find Suitable Franchises

When looking for franchise opportunities there are two different marketing sectors to look at: 1) Specialist Franchise Media 2) Non Franchise Media.

Within each different sector there are a wide range of places to look and these are often broken down into:

- Online Media
- Printed Media
- Exhibitions
- Word of Mouth
- Franchise Broker

Buying a Franchise: The Process

The process for buying any franchise is relatively similar. At every step of the franchise recruitment process it is important to remember that the onus is on you to do your own due diligence and to check that information you are provided with is accurate and that you are suitable as a franchisee.

The franchisor is not allowed to falsify or deliberately provide misinformation, however there are many ways to provide information in a creative way! When buying a franchise there are typically seven steps people go through:

- Getting basic information on the franchise
- Registering an interest in the franchise
- An interview with the franchisor
- Assessing the suitability of the franchise
- The franchise offer
- Understanding the Franchise Agreement
- Signing the Franchise Agreement

Conclusion

Franchising offers and can provide excellent opportunities to own and run a proven business with the support and guidance of an established business owner. The franchise industry in the UK is well established and there are around 1,000 franchises for people to choose from covering virtually every business sector and industry specialism.

Although the UK does not have any specific franchise legislation there is an established support industry to help prospective franchisees make the right choice. This support includes a franchisor membership scheme operated by the British Franchise Association, advice from High Street Banks with specialist Franchise departments, and specialist franchise solicitors to advice on Franchise Agreements.

In addition, although there is a support industry for prospective franchisees to call upon, ultimately the success of any franchise will be down to the hard work and dedication of the franchisee. There is no guarantee as to the profits a franchisee will make and therefore the onus is on every prospective franchisee to do their own due diligence on the franchise opportunity BEFORE they buy. Running any business, regardless as to whether it is a franchise business or not, is a big commitment and requires a lot of hard work. Having said this however owning a business can be extremely rewarding both financially and personally.

In the remaining chapters of this book, we have included case studies of women that have bought franchises. We have also included a "Glossary of Terms" to help you understand some of the language used in franchising.

Finally we have included a list of "sources of help" which includes contact details for the British Franchise Association, the High Street Franchise Banks, the Franchise Exhibition Organisers and the main Franchise Media providers.

PART 2

FRANCHISING & YOU
by Murielle Maupoint

CHAPTER 6

Is franchising the right business model for me?

So you're considering taking your financial destiny into your own hands. The craving for self-employment and the desire to run your own business may have been knocking around in your head for years, maybe even decades by now, or you may have simply reached that stage of discontent with the status quo and be looking for a change and a new challenge. Perhaps your personal circumstances lend themselves to you having the flexibility of self-employment rather than working for someone else? Perhaps you want the freedom to make your own decisions and to be directly rewarded for your efforts? Whatever your reasons are for considering running your own business, you now find yourself increasingly compelled to explore all the possibilities.

Why Do I Want To Run My Own Business?

Before you embark on the exciting rollercoaster of self-employment, it is useful to start by checking your motivation for doing so. In the world of Dragons Den, The Apprentice and other such TV shows that exhalt the virtues of entrepreneurship and self-employment, it can all seem very sexy and glamorous. Indeed, in many respects, entrepreneurs have become the 'rock stars' of the 21st century. Why wouldn't you want a piece of that action? The sports cars, private jets, luxury homes and Caribbean hideaways... Many people launch their self-employment careers on the illusion of big business, but what is the reality?

The truth is that whilst the potential for multi-million pound success exists, those who make it BIG are few and far between. The majority of people, in whatever field you explore, will be ticking along, keeping their head just above water.

Running your own business is not an easy option to make big money. For many people they are simply buying themselves a job with the added headache of being the one ultimately responsible for everything and managing the ups and downs of business life. Being self-employed never stops – it has the capacity to be all consuming 24/7, 365 days a year – because, even if you are not physically working 'in' the business you will need to be working 'on' the business.

So, do you still think running your own business is the right option for you?

Yes, I know that there are many disadvantages to working for someone else but let's face it, for most people, when you balance things out, it can also be relatively easy:

- You get told what to do and when to do it
- You get your pay cheque at regular intervals and might even get a bonus for a job well done
- You get time off for holidays and you get paid if you are off work sick
- You work your set number of hours and at the end of the working day, you can go home and forget about it all.

Sounds pretty good! So why would you want to run your own business?

Here's the thing, despite the advantages of being employed, owning your own business can be an amazingly rewarding experience. It's never easy but the pride, the sense of achievement and personal fulfilment you can get from being able to take control of your destiny is incredible. And for many people it can be a truly transformational experience – showing you the courage, creativity and resilience that you possess but were never aware of.

There are many reasons for wanting to run your own business the consequences of which may have a positive or negative impact on your intrinsic motivation.

I want to make a fortune – money as a primary motivational driver can create great energy for action, but there may also be some negative consequences. What happens to your motivation for action if you consistently don't make the money you aspire to? Also how realistic is it that your small business will become a multi-million pound empire? It happens for some but not many!

I want the freedom – the truth is that being self-employed can be more restrictive than being employed. For many small business owners they have to run their life around their business and customer's needs.

I want an easier life – in most cases running your own business will bring a level of complexity and challenge to your life that you never imagined! Running your own business, especially in the early days, is likely to push you way outside your comfort zone!

No one else will employ me – Is this really true? No one? Maybe you need to up-skill or re-skill yourself? Starting a business because you think you can't get a job may not always be the right motivation. That being said, many people have started very successful businesses on the back of a lack of perceived alternative possibilities.

I don't want to be accountable to anyone – whatever you do in life you will be accountable to someone. Even as a franchisee you will be accountable to others, such as your customers, bank managers and franchisor.

I want to do what I want when I want – it is possible to run a business around your needs enabling you to have a certain amount of flexibility. However, if you are running a service in which customers have certain expectations, then you will need to do certain things at certain times.

I want the power and status – in some societies there is a level of kudos associated with running your own business. Power and status can certainly come on the back of running a business well but they shouldn't necessarily be your driving force for doing it.

I want to prove something to someone else – whenever we decide to do something to prove something to someone else then we are in some respects disempowering ourselves. This is because our motivation for action sits outside ourselves – rather than it being intrinsic (naturally occurring inside our self). Indeed, I know of someone who was desperate to run a successful business to show their father that they were a success. She spent every hour of the day working hard on the business – unfortunately her father died before her business became profitable and she was left with a gaping hole in her motivation. You see he had been her driving force and now he was no longer there the juice had fizzled out of her ambition.

I want to meet others' expectations of me – sometimes there are expectations thrust upon us by others, especially family members. For some families running your own business is the 'family business' and it takes a lot of personal strength to break free from that if it is not something that is in your heart to do.

I want to challenge and develop myself – running your own business will present countless opportunities for you to develop your skills and your self. An attitude of learning, change and curiosity is therefore essential to your business success.

I want to make a difference and to do something that serves others – the business people, who offer something that is truly of value, to someone else, will always succeed. Be of service to others and you will reap the rewards. Business should always be about your customers rather than about you!

I want to work hard to make my dreams come true – it is important to have a dream and even more important to take action towards realising it! Running a successful business requires the consistent application of work. Expect to work hard and smart and be very clear about the goals you will need to achieve to make your dream come true.

I want to be responsible for my financial destiny – in a modern day economy where jobs are no longer for life, running your own business can be a viable option for many – enabling them to take control of their professional and financial future. A great sense of personal stability can come from knowing you are in charge of your financial future.

I have an inexplicable force within me that drives and inspires me to do it – when you feel something is your 'calling' then it's a very different quality of drive and motivation. It's an itch that needs to be scratched and only by you doing that which you are inspired to do will you satisfy that itch. Great personal fulfilment can come from listening to your 'calling'.

It doesn't really matter why you want to run your own business as long as you are very honest with yourself and clear about the motivational forces driving your decision. Any motivational driver that is external to you, in other words sits outside of your control, for instance: to meet the expectations of others, will be influenced by outside forces and therefore ultimately is outside of your control. Any motivational drivers that are based on elusive, ambiguous concepts such as freedom and success can also create issues. After all what is freedom? How do you measure success?

These things can be an outcome of running your own business but ideally should not be the driving force. Ideally, you want the driving force for your self-employment decision to be based on your intrinsic motivation and things that are realistic and within your control. Running your own business has the potential to transform your life and empower you in ways you never imagined – just make sure your motivation is right from the outset as you will need it to drive you through the dark nights of business ownership!

What Are The Different Options Open To Me?

You have done a little bit of honest self-reflection and have decided that running your own business is the right thing for you – offering you the potential for an incredibly rewarding experience on all levels – financial, professional and personal. Broadly speaking there are three ways you can bring your business ownership dreams to life. You can:

- Start a new business
- Buy an existing business
- Invest in a franchise business

Each of these options has their own distinct advantages and disadvantages and can be more suited to some people than others. Let's explore each of these options further...

Start a New Business

Here you find yourself with a business idea, something ideally that is completely new or brings a new twist to an existing concept. Equally, it could be an existing business concept that you are bringing to a new location or to satisfy demand in an area. Either way, in this scenario, you have decided to start something completely new and will therefore need to go through the process of any business start-up including:

- Creating a business plan

- Finding a business name & creating a brand for the business
- Obtaining finance
- Meeting all legal obligations i.e. registering for self-employment, company registration, planning applications, health & safety certifications
- Setting up all business systems including accounting
- Purchasing supplies and equipment
- Marketing the service/product effectively
- Finding and retaining customers
- Servicing your customers' needs

And the list goes on...

For the more creative, independent and entrepreneurially minded amongst us, starting something from nothing can be an exhilarating experience. Offering you the scope to create something that is completely bespoke and true to you and your vision. However, an independent, new business is most often based on both an untried idea and an untested operation. Business start-ups therefore come with a big risk and a very high failure rate, with as many as one in three failing in their first three years in the UK. That being said, for every one business that fails, another two survive with some even going on to be very successful. Every successful business starts somewhere!

Buy an Existing Business

If the idea of starting a new business feels too risky then you can always explore the option of buying an existing business as a going concern. There are thousands of business owners who for one reason or another are seeking to dispose of their business. The advantage of buying a going concern is that the business is already set up – all the initial set-up work has been done for you and hopefully the business comes with a well-established client base and sound financials that you can take over. Once you own the business you can always make some tweaks and adjustments to suit your taste – although be careful not to tamper with it too much if the model is working well!

If you do explore buying an existing business then make sure you do your research carefully. It never ceases to amaze me the lack of detail and poor quality of financial information provided by some businesses seeking a new owner. Don't just look at the figures that are there but use your common sense to question the figures that aren't there. Are they showing all the costs involved in running the business? Staffing costs? Accountancy? Insurance? Provisions for liabilities? etc.

Don't just work from the profit & loss statement, make sure you get hold of the full set of accounts over a period of at least 3 years (if the business has been running for that long) so you can also explore any trends or patterns in the operations of the business. Also visit the business at different times of the day/week to check that what the current business owners are saying about the business reflects what is actually happening in practice.

Invest in a Franchise

The fact that you are reading this book indicates that you are already keen to explore the opportunities offered by investing in a franchise and hopefully the information you glean from these pages will help you to make the right decision for you. An advantage of buying a business format franchise is that, like the going concern business option above, someone has already done all the initial hard work for you. The franchisor has set up a business with everything that is needed for it to function. They have tested that the business model works and they are granting you the right to operate an extension of that business.

When you invest in a franchise, you get the right to use the name of the business, sell its products/services and deliver the business using their operating, marketing, management methods and technical expertise. It is your business and you are ultimately accountable for its performance but you must deliver that business according to the specifications set by the franchisor. You should receive extensive training and support by the franchisor to ensure that you are successful at running the business. Essentially, franchising offers you a 'business in a box'. For this reason, investing in a franchise can be a very solid way forward for some people. While Domino Pizza, Rosemary Conley and Dyno Rod are familiar names, franchises are available in pretty much every possible field you could imagine, including: business services, beauty & health, catering, home improvement, printing, publishing, sports, children and travel. The number of active franchises identified by the NatWest/BFA Survey 2012 was 929 with an estimated annual sector turnover of £13.4 billion employing nearly 600,000 people. Most importantly, the number of franchisees reporting profitability in the survey was 91% - which is pretty impressive considering the current economic climate. Consequently, 81% of franchisees believed that they had a competitive advantage as a result of running a franchised business over other small businesses.

Risk vs Certainty

Whichever path you choose towards business ownership there is always a certain level of risk involved. Indeed, the only certainty that exists is that some businesses will fail and some will succeed. When it comes to women though, it is widely touted that women are more financially risk averse than their male counterparts – preferring to save rather than invest. I don't know whether this belief is true. What I do know is that the more women buy into that belief then the more risk averse women can become. Could the foundations of this widespread belief simply be that women typically have less funds in the bank than men and therefore have less money that they are willing or able to risk? Let's face it if you don't have much in the first place then you are bound to be more cautious about what you do with it – regardless of your gender!

From a business model perspective, starting your own business from nothing comes with the greatest level of risk. Remember, 1 in 3 new businesses go out of business within the first three years. If that happened to your business, could you bounce back? What would be the long-term personal, professional and financial impact of having your business fail? Whilst I want you to be excited about the possibility of venturing into the world of business ownership, this is something that must be considered with a healthy dose of self-honesty and realism. Business failure doesn't just happen to other people – for a whole manner of reasons it could happen to you too!

If the risks associated with starting a business from scratch are too high for you then taking over a going concern or a franchised business model may be a better option for you. With the business foundations in place and a history and brand to take advantage of, investing in an existing business or franchise can minimise the risks associated with business ownership. The key word here though is MINIMISE! Just because a business already exists or the business model has been franchised doesn't give you any certainty of success. Nothing does! Buying into an existing business or franchise simply means that you may be more likely to succeed. A final point to consider is just because someone has franchised their business model or is selling their existing business; it doesn't mean that it will be a successful business for you!

An Overview of Options

When considering which business option is best for you, it is useful to look at the differences between each model and what each offers. Please note that each business is different and so the following table offers a quick general point of information only in relation to each business option highlighted:

	New Start-Up	Going Concern	Franchise
Level of Business Risk	Higher	Moderate	Lower
Business Support & Training	None (can access through external providers)	Minimal (can access through external providers)	Higher
Level of Independence	Higher	Moderate	Lower
Ability to Make Decisions	All Yours	All Yours – but may be constrained by historical success	Locally Yours – Globally/ Strategically franchisor
Ability to Offer Creative Input	Higher	Moderate to High	Lower
Use of Established Systems	None	Yes (but will also vary depending on the offering)	Yes (will vary across offerings but systems potentially tested across number of sites)
Direct Benefits to Business Owner	All For Yourself	All For Yourself	For Yourself & franchisor
Working on a Day to Day Basis	By Yourself	By Yourself	By Yourself but Part of Bigger Network

The Disadvantages of Buying a Franchise

There are clear advantages and disadvantages to investing in any type of business model. With respect to franchising there are some factors that could be perceived as a disadvantage for some people. Let's explore them...

You Must Follow the System: It's simple, when you invest in a business format franchise, you are buying a set 'recipe' that offers you the potential to achieve a specific outcome if you follow that specific recipe. If you start tampering with the recipe then the business outcomes become unpredictable.

The only way the franchise model can work across a number of different franchise units is by ensuring that each franchisee follows the system they have invested in. Remember this point; if you invest in a franchise then you are paying money to a franchisor to follow 'their' system. Why in that case would you want to tinker with it? If there are things you don't like about the system that you are considering investing in then that franchise is NOT for you! End of story, don't invest in it.

The whole notion of business format franchising is that you are buying into how someone else does something successfully. Therefore you must follow that system to the letter – from the goods and services they sell, where they buy their supplies from to the colour of the paint on the walls! This means that you have a complete lack of independence as to how the business is delivered. This definitely won't suit the more entrepreneurially minded person but will be great for people who want an established and successful system to follow.

Initial & On-Going Costs: In order to become the proud owner of a franchise business you will need to part with some of your hard earned cash. Depending on the type of franchise you invest in, the initial franchise investment fee could be as low as several thousand pounds, or as high as hundreds of thousands.

Upon closer inspection, in some cases you may find that the costs of buying a franchise are more than if you went ahead and set up a similar business on your own. What you must remember is that when you invest in a franchise you are not only buying the branding, equipment, training, etc. but also a range of intangibles such as brand awareness, tried and tested systems, business support, collective buying power as well as the intellectual capital and experience of the franchisor.

All in all you may find that whilst more expensive than starting something similar from scratch, the increased chance of success makes investing in a franchise a worthwhile expenditure. Aside from the initial franchise fee, there will also be other costs to be paid, such as the monthly management and marketing fees and franchise renewal fees.

Being Part of a Network: How may you ask is being part of a franchise network a disadvantage? Well consider this... what happens if a franchisee in another part of a country does something that receives bad publicity? What might the impact of that be on your business and the overall brand of the franchise? As a franchisee you are part and parcel of a bigger entity. If something affects one of you, it has the capacity to affect all of you! You are part of a bigger network of franchisees and the potential exists, however slim, for everyone to be tainted with the same brush.

Future Disposal: Any sensible person investing in a business needs to think about exit strategies from the outset. In other words, how can I dispose of this business should I wish to do so in the future. Let's face it, people change and in the future you might decide to move abroad, retire or focus on something completely different.

If you have set up your own business from scratch then you can do what you want with it, whenever you want to. As a franchisee however, you will be held under the terms of the franchise agreement, which may or may not dictate how you can dispose of the franchise. Let's say you decide you want to sell your franchise as a going concern and recoup some of your investment. Well, most circumstances, you will find that the franchisor has to approve any potential re-sale of your franchise, which could slow matters down for you and limit your options!

No Guarantee of Success: Finally, the truth is that however well established the franchise is that you are considering buying or however much it has its finger on the pulse of what consumers want – there is still no absolute guarantee of success. You are buying a recipe not an outcome! And that recipe may not have been fully tested by the franchisor! Moreover, any number of factors could impact the projections that you based your decision to buy the franchise on: a downturn in the economy, a public health concern (i.e. horsemeat found in burgers), ineffective business systems and of course your own failings as a business owner.

Ultimately, there is no guarantee of success. You will still have to work very hard to make your business profitable and successful. And even if your business succeeds there are no guarantees that your franchisor might not go out of business.

The Advantages of Buying a Franchise

Ok, now that you are clear as to what some of the disadvantages of investing in a franchise are, let's turn to the positives associated with the franchise business model.

Lower Risk: Starting a new business is risky business. One of the primary reasons why people are drawn to the idea of buying a franchise is that the risks of business failure are perceived to be lower than that for other business options. The whole essence of franchising is that you are buying a 'tried and tested' business model with proven results. That should in theory significantly reduce the risk of your business failing and maximise its chances of success. With 33% businesses failing within 3 years of start-up, launching your business on the back of a proven model can be a massive advantage. Indeed, the NatWest/BFA Survey 2011 estimated that the overall franchisee 'churn' was less than 9%. Of this figure only 3.1% was down to financial failure with the remaining factors for churn down to business dispute (0.8%), retirement (1.1%), personal circumstances (1.4%) and other (2.4%).

Proven Model: The greatest benefit of investing in a franchise is that you are buying an established and 'proven' business model. In other words, the franchisor has gone through the pain of setting up the business and they are offering you a template for success to replicate in your own territory. A sound franchise proposition should have run the business over a number of years and during that time refined the business model and overcome all the reasons businesses typically fail such as:

- Poor marketing
- Lack of understanding of customer needs
- Poor cash flow management and ineffective financial accounting
- Failure to create a business plan
- Inefficient supply chain

- Insufficient finances
- Failure to keep up with new developments
- Poor location
- Poor management systems

The primary reason that the new business failure rate is so high is because the owners have to go through the learning curve associated with operating every aspect of that specific type business. Franchising reduces that learning curve substantially. Just think what an advantage this is – someone sharing with you the recipe to their success!

Support & Training: You should expect to receive lots of support, training and advice from your franchisor regarding every aspect of the business. Remember they want you to succeed. Your success directly impacts their success and their financial bottom line. Typically you will find that a franchise can be purchased by people who have no knowledge of that business industry.

The franchisor provides all the necessary training, support, systems and back-up to ensure that the new franchisee can successfully operate their franchise. This package of support means that you could invest in any type of business available as a franchise as the franchisor will teach you everything you need to know to get going. Talk about opening up new opportunities for you! Clearly, the more complex or technical the business concept you are investing in then the more training and support you can expect.

Problem Solving: Being a franchisee means that you automatically become part of an experienced network (the size of the network will vary depending on how many franchise units are in operation) that understands your business and can therefore help you effectively problem solve situations as they arise. The experience of the franchisor's management team and operational franchisees increases the potential for your success. You can be pretty much guaranteed that within a well-established franchise network, any problem you encounter will have been encountered before and solved by someone else already. Think about how powerful that is – having access to a massive resource of knowledge about the ins and outs of the business you are operating in.

Research & Buying Power: For any business to succeed it must keep costs down and continue to innovate to keep up with the changing needs of customers. By being part of a franchise network you can benefit from the economies of scale created by the collective purchasing power of all the franchisees. Of course this will mean that you can't go off and buy your own supplies but then why would you want to if you can get good quality, lower priced goods through your franchise network? Equally, when you are running a business on your own you often don't have enough time to do everything that needs to be done today let alone invest time in new and/or improved products/services for the future. By being part of the franchise network, the franchisor can continue to research and innovate new offerings and pass on the final products/services for you to deliver locally within your franchise. In this way your offering continues to remain fresh and viable and responsive to customer needs in the changing business landscape.

Access to Finance: Every business will need investment of some kind to get it off the ground. Even a web-based business needs some funding to buy domain names, develop the brand, etc. Many people, and especially women, will finance their new business through their own personal savings, or by re-mortgaging their home or seeking investment from friends and family. In some circumstances though, you may wish to access commercial finance to fund the launch of your business.

If you do not have a track record in the industry or the necessary collateral it can be very difficult and time consuming to secure finance. This is where investing in a franchise can also come into its own. Some franchisors have already had their franchise offering pre-approved for lending by specific banks. This means that with the support of your franchisor and a good business plan, you can often access the required funding far more quickly than in other circumstances. After all, you are requesting a loan based on a proven business model.

If the risks are lower for you as a business owner then they are also lower for the banks. Naturally, you as the franchisee must still accept responsibility for the loan, but the franchisor's involvement can increase the likelihood that a loan will be approved.

Branding & Marketing: If you have ever previously set up a business you know how time consuming and demoralising it can be trying to find a name for your business and creating a great brand around it. With more and more businesses out there it sometimes feels like all the good names have already been taken! Another advantage of investing in a franchise is that you are buying an already 'branded' business. Depending on the franchise, the brand may enjoy regional, national or even international customer recognition. Clearly not all franchises are as well-known as McDonalds but in general, being able to use a recognised trademark and brand name increases your selling power. Of course for that brand to build its power, you and your franchisor must continually invest in marketing and advertising.

Again, by being part of a franchise network, you can contribute towards a bigger, national or regional marketing campaign that otherwise you as an independent business may not have been able to afford. Equally when it comes to local marketing, you can tap into the collective experience and intelligence of your franchise network to make sure your advertising spend is effective.

All the above factors therefore contribute towards the fact that investing in a franchise can offer you an improved chance of success compared to other business models. The nature of franchising means that you can benefit from a tried and tested successful business model. However, just because the model increases your chances of success it doesn't mean that it is the right model for you. In the next chapter we shall explore a number of factors that may or may not predispose you to being a great franchisee!

CHAPTER 7

Would I make a great franchisee?

Many people dream of running their own business but not everyone has the necessary skills and personality to be a successful franchisee. Even though odds are stacked in your favour when you invest in a franchise, there are still some key factors that predispose some people to being more successful, as a franchisee and/or business owner, than others.

When you attend an interview with a franchisor they will be keen to check that you have the right mix of skills, attitude and experience to ensure you have the highest possibility of success in delivering their franchise.

This chapter therefore will provide you with the opportunity to quickly reflect on who you are and what your skills are in order for you to assess whether you have what it takes to run a successful business and be a great franchisee.

Whilst as individuals we are all different, there are certain qualities that every great business person needs to succeed:

Motivation & Drive – you need to be a self-starter and to be able to motivate yourself on a daily basis to start and complete the tasks that are required of you. If you need someone else telling you what to do all the time or 'cleaning up after you' then running your own business may not be a wise move! It is the motivation and inner drive that you possess that you will need to rely on to get up and go on cold wet winter mornings even when you feel less than your best.

Determination & Persistence – as you run your own business you will face lots of challenges. It is important that you are able to meet those challenges head on and to have the determination to persist. There are some months when customers and cash flow may completely dry up and everything that could go wrong does go wrong. The measure of a true business person is persisting in the face of adversity.

Decisiveness & Assertiveness – as a business owner you must be able to make decisions, often with very little information. You must be prepared to back your decisions and accept that whatever decision you make now is based on what you know at the time. If you are the type of person that needs to know everything in advance and be 100% certain that you are making the right decision before making a decision then you may struggle as a business owner.

Common Sense – this is a really under-rated quality and one that I think is often in very short supply! If you are endowed with a healthy dose of common sense then you will be able to see solutions and opportunities in the midst of the biggest problems and challenges you face.

People Skills – people buy from people. For you to be a successful business owner you need to have the people skills to enable you to build rapport and communicate effectively with your customers, suppliers and franchisor. Business is all about relationships and creating connections – as a woman you have a natural tendency towards being a great rapport builder.

Organisational Skills – a fundamental business skill is being organised and being able to arrange your work and time to achieve the tasks that are required at any given time. If you struggle getting organised then perhaps you are better suited to working for someone that tells you what to do and when. Maybe you have been out of work for some time and are doubting your skills? If you run a home and a family well then I can guarantee that you have great organisational skills!

Optimistic & Realistic – it is important for every business owner to have a dream and vision. You need a healthy dose of optimism to help you through the dark times however this must be carefully balanced with realism to ensure that you don't delude yourself about what is actually going on around you. Many businesses fail because their owners bury their heads in the sand and don't look at the reality of the situation.

Support – every successful business person has an effective support network. Your support network could include your family, friends, business professionals such as accountants, business coaches, etc. and of course your franchisor and the franchise network! Please make sure your support network doesn't consist of just 'yes' people who will agree with everything you say. You need people in your support network that will be honest with you and help you face up to some harsh realities at times. Do not underestimate how important it is to have your partner and/or family's support. Especially, in the early days, your business will consume a lot of your time and this will have an impact on those closest to you. If those closest to you don't support you then this is likely to have a negative impact on your ability to perform to your highest potential in the business. Get everyone on-board from the outset with your business plans and you will have an easier ride. And who knows they may enjoy helping you out too.

Jack of All Trades – running your own business requires that you are able and willing to pull your sleeves up and do everything that is required of you to service your customers and exceed their expectations. You must be prepared to work 'in' as well as 'on' the business. What do I mean by that? You will need to do the day to day delivery of the front facing business and also all the background tasks which could include a whole range of things such as administration, bookkeeping, accounting, cold-calling, quotes, tendering, marketing, advertising, staff training, quality assurance.... the list goes on. As you read the case studies in the next section you will begin to appreciate just how critical and time consuming all these background activities are. Indeed, especially in the early days you may need to say good-bye to your evenings and weekends. Are you willing to do what it takes to run a successful business or are there aspects that fill you with horror? Do you hate numbers? Does the prospect of picking up the phone and making cold-calls fill you with dread? And if there are aspects of running the business that you are not comfortable with, have you budgeted within your business plan for someone else to undertake that function i.e. bookkeeping, for you?

Confidence & Self-Belief – to be a successful business owner you need to have a certain level of confidence and self-belief. It isn't prudent to invest in a franchise or any other business with an underlying fear that you might not be able to make it work. One of the reasons I am so keen to encourage women into business ownership is the massive impact it can have on their self-esteem and confidence. There is nothing quite like running your own business to help you appreciate the vast reservoir of skills you possess and boost your confidence and self-belief through the roof! And if your confidence is perhaps struggling a little then you can always get some coaching or therapy to give you the boost you need. If it didn't work the world's greatest sports stars, celebrities, business people and politicians wouldn't use Coaches!

The above 'qualities' and factors are some of the things that every great business owner needs to give themselves the best chance of success. However, a great franchisee needs all of the above and more! So let's discover if you have what it takes to be a great franchisee?

Can I Follow a Set System?

The hallmark of being a great franchisee is the ability to follow a set system and instructions. For you to deliver a brilliant franchised business you need to follow the Franchise Operating Manual and the instructions contained therein. You cannot pick and choose what you want to do or like doing and change the things that you don't. So ask yourself:

- Are you happiest following instructions or do you prefer being able to do your own thing?
- Do you tend to see how to make things better and want to change things or do you prefer to go with how things are?
- Do you like being able to apply your own personal touch to things or do you prefer fitting in with something that already exists?

You need to be really honest with yourself here. If you are someone with an entrepreneurial mind-set that likes to change things, innovate and do your own thing then franchising is definitely not for you. I am happy to admit that I would make a terrible franchisee and would drive my franchisor insane with my continuous desire to change and improve their system.

Do I Want to Be Part of a Team?

Do you prefer to work on your own or as part of a team? The beauty of franchising is that you work for yourself but you are not by yourself. You have access to a broader network of support, advice, guidance and technical expertise related to every aspect of the business. The franchisor and the franchise network are there to help you to be successful. So if you are someone who wants to be your own boss but would really appreciate back-up support then franchising may well be for you. Depending on the type of franchise you decide to invest in you may also find yourself managing your own team.

Am I Happy Being an Owner but Not the Creator?

Some people want to own their own business for all the kudos that comes with developing something from scratch and for the ability to continually innovate and develop the business. As a franchisee you must be happy owning the business and running it according to the franchisor's vision and plan. There are many advantages to not being the creator – most importantly that someone else has gone through the pain of setting up a business, made mistakes and rectified them such that you have a template for success to work from. Yes, you may be able to make suggestions for improvement to the franchisor but you must accept that they are under no requirement to implement those suggestions. Franchising can offer the right person the best of both worlds – your own business without the pain and costly mistakes associated with starting/running something on your own.

Do I Enjoy Learning?

As a franchisee you have the potential to invest in a business in a completely different field to that which you have any skills or previous experience of. Indeed, many franchisors prefer recruiting people who are completely inexperienced in the business so they can train them to deliver the business completely in line with the Franchise Operating Manual.

This opens up huge possibilities for you to invest in a business, in an area you may never have dreamed of, and equally it could give you a strong footing in an industry you would love to work in but that without the necessary experience and skills, employers would not have considered you. In this sense, the world is your oyster. You can become a franchisee in any area you like on the condition that you are happy to learn and to receive extensive training. The intensity and length of that training will depend on the complexity of the franchise you are investing in. If you enjoy learning and are open to being taught then you could make a very good franchisee.

Also remember that as a new business owner, the learning curve will be steep, so it is essential for you to have an open mind, to be open to making mistakes as you learn and to be happy asking questions. Indeed, for you to get the most out of your training and set your franchise up on the best footing, you need to be prepared to ask your franchisor lots and lots of questions. Remember your franchisor doesn't know whether you know something or not – it's your responsibility to tell them and to ensure that the training meets your needs.

As a franchisee you will find that every day provides you with new opportunities to learn and to grow not only your business but you as an individual. Can you embrace an attitude of continuous learning?

How Do I Feel About Being Monitored?

When you set up your own business you don't usually answer to anyone (well expect the bank manager...). As a franchisee you will be answerable to the franchisor who will monitor your business activities closely to ensure that you are following their business model and the processes/procedures set out in the Franchise Operating Manual. It is in their interest and in the interest of your business long-term success that you follow the system.

As a franchisee you will therefore be expected to follow the monitoring systems implemented by the franchisor and that will include submitting reports, financial data and other types of paperwork at key intervals throughout the year. To help you stay on track, your franchisor will give you feedback and it is their right to ask you to make changes in specific areas to ensure you comply with their franchise system. It is important that you are open to receiving such feedback and constructive criticism. Your franchisor is experienced at running this business so their support and guidance is invaluable to your success – this is part of what you will be paying for. If you don't like someone 'looking over your shoulder' or being accountable to someone else for how you run your business then you might struggle as a franchisee.

Are You Ready to Make a Commitment?

Typically when you sign a Franchise Agreement it will be for an initial period of 5 years. This means that you are contractually and legally obliged to run the business for that length of time. Depending on which franchise you invest in, you may have performance targets that your business must meet every month or quarter... so you can't peddle at your own pace. If the idea of committing to something for at least 5 years fills you with doubt or dread then investing in a franchise may not be the best choice for you.

Be very clear about what you are prepared to commit to before you sign on the dotted line! Remember that as a franchisee it may not be that easy to dispose of your business and in any case depending on the economic climate you may struggle to find someone to take over the business for you. As part of the commitment you make to the franchisor you may find that the agreement prevents you from being involved in any other business activities. This is understandable, the franchisor wants you to focus all your attention and energy on making the business a success and this might prove difficult if your focus was diluted with other business activities. So are you prepared to run your franchise for a minimum of 5 years to the exclusion of any other activities or opportunities that may present themselves along the way? If so, you're well on your way to being a great franchisee!

Quick Franchisee Checklist

As we have just seen, there are many qualities that enhance your chances of success as a business owner and in particular a franchisee. So do you have what it takes to make a great franchisee?

- I am motivated, determined and driven to succeed
- I am a people person and have good communication skills
- I enjoy following instructions and working within a set system
- I love the idea of working for myself and being part of a bigger team
- I am well organised and can manage my time/workload effectively
- I am keen to roll my sleeves up and do everything required to make my business a success
- I have the confidence and self-belief to make my business a success

- I am really open to feedback and constructive criticism
- Having a franchisor to support me is really comforting
- I love learning and the thought of being trained to do something new and run my own business fills me with excitement
- I want to hit the ground running and spend my time running a business rather than setting it up from scratch
- I am ready to commit the next 5 years of my life and probably more to running my own business

If by reading this chapter you have identified areas where you feel you may struggle as a business owner or franchisee then please don't despair just yet. The point of this exercise is for you to appreciate some of the key qualities and attributes linked to business success and for you to recognise any areas of weakness that exist for you. Armed with this knowledge you can take appropriate action to remedy any such weakness either through training, coaching or professional support. There is a wealth of support out there to help you succeed if you are willing to access it. And if you have ticked most of the boxes in the above **Quick Franchisee Checklist** then you know you are well on your way to making a great franchisee. The next step is working out what type of franchise would be right for you.

CHAPTER 8

What type of franchise would be best for me?

With over 900 different active franchises to choose from in the UK (2012) alone, covering pretty much every imaginable industry (see the Franchise Industry Sectors Chapter), it can be an overwhelming task to determine which franchise opportunity is right for you. Some people become a franchisee down to what can only be called 'fate', some find their perfect franchise through extensive research and others benefit from the expertise of franchise search services to match them to their franchise. There is no right or wrong way to find your perfect franchise.

What is most important is determining the key factors that will influence the type of franchise you gravitate towards. Please use the questions in this chapter to reflect on who you are, your personal circumstances and needs before you even start exploring franchises. The more you know yourself and what you are after, the more likely you will be to find the right franchise for you and just as importantly to know what you don't want! So let's begin...

What Is Really Important to Me?

Our lives and how we function in this world are driven by our core values – the things that are important to us. Running your own business offers you a great opportunity to align your core values with the work that you do. When for most people work takes up the largest part of their waking day, I believe it is critical to find something to do that you love and that resonates with your core values. Why? Because when you align your values with what you do, you will not only find what you do easier but you will enjoy it more too! So take a few moments to clear your mind and then ask yourself:

'What is important to me about running my own business?'

Now jot down all the things that start spinning round your mind. Write down absolutely everything that comes to you:

You will most likely find that a dozen or so 'values' quickly pop into your head and then your mind goes blank... just take a deep breath and ask yourself:

'What else is important to me about running my own business?'

Again jot down everything that springs to mind:

Now from the above lists I want you to choose the top 5 things that you **must have** when running your own business. There is no right or wrong answer – these are your personal values that are important to you in the context of running your business. Someone else may have a completely different list and that is OK. Your number 1 value must be the one that you simply cannot do without. So go on, have a look at your lists from above and choose 5 and put them in order of priority below:

My Top 5 Values

1...

2...

3...

4...

5...

Whatever your top 5 values are, this is the list that will underpin your successful matchmaking with a specific franchise offering. You must make sure that the franchise you choose satisfies those top 5 values. Let's assume that your top 5 are:

- Flexibility
- Time with Family
- Personal Satisfaction
- Money
- Fun

You need to make sure that the franchise you are considering offers you the opportunity to meet those values. For instance, if the franchise tied you to working 9-5, Monday – Friday, 48 weeks per year then your value of **Flexibility** and possibly **Time with Family** would not be met. In such a scenario, it would not be sensible to continue exploring that option despite how much money you might make since **Money** is much lower down on the list of the values in this example. Equally, you might find a franchise that offers you plenty of **Flexibility** and a decent income (**Money**) but it would be the equivalent of watching paint drying – with the values of **Personal Satisfaction** and **Fun** being compromised. In such an example, this too would not be a suitable franchise opportunity.

Am I More of an Introvert or Extrovert? If you are someone who can naturally recharge your batteries, when you are exhausted, in the company of others then you may be more suited to franchises that involve interacting with groups of people. So choose something that gives you the opportunity to interact with others as opposed to condemning you to a life sat in your home office on your own. Equally, if your tendency is towards introversion then it's probably best for you not to invest in a children's party entertainment franchise where you need to fancy dress, sing and clown around in front of groups of children and their parents!

Am I Good With People? Any business you invest in will have some contact with people – be it customers, suppliers or your franchisor. If you are good with people then it will be in your interest to choose a franchise that allows you to take centre stage and exercise that gift. On the other hand, if you struggle to deal with people then choose a franchise that limits your direct contact with people.

Am I More Proactive or Reactive? If you are proactive then go for a franchise that gives you the opportunity to exercise your 'get up and go'. If you have a more reactive nature then choose something where people come to you or perhaps there is a central booking call centre that directs enquiries to you rather than expecting you to make cold calls to recruit new customers.

What Skills Do I Enjoy Using? Owning your own franchise gives you the opportunity to exercise all your skills however each franchise will be more suited towards a certain set of skills as opposed to others. So write down all the skills you really enjoy using – think of everything: talking to people, fixing things, solving problems, listening, motivating people, organising people, managing projects...

Now create a list of what you believe are your top 10 skills. It will be really useful for you to have been through this exercise as any franchisor will want to know what you are good at! It is also a great opportunity for you to make sure there is a good fit between the great skills that you have and what skills will benefit the business you are investing in.

My Top 10 Skills

1..

2..

3..

4..

5..

6..

7..

8..

9..

10..

A quick final word on skills – a lack of skills is not a block to owning a specific franchise since your franchisor will give you appropriate training for you to run the business successfully. However if there is a skill you love using then you owe it to yourself to ensure the franchise opportunity offers you the potential to use it. Equally, if you hate finances and numbers then please don't invest in a bookkeeping business! However much training you receive from the franchisor, if being good with numbers is not your thing then don't put yourself through that misery!

Have I Got Good Attention to Detail? Some people have a natural ability to focus on the details of whatever they are involved in. Others prefer dealing with more abstract concepts and the bigger picture. If your natural preference is towards working with the detail then choose a franchise opportunity that relies on that attention to detail and accuracy to be successful. If on the other hand, your natural tendency is towards the big picture then spare yourself the pain of investing in a franchise that requires you to examine minute details.

Do I Enjoy the Stability of Doing the Same Thing or Do I Prefer Variety in my Working Life? If having variety in what you do is important to you then make sure you get that within the day to day franchise offering you are investing in otherwise you will become bored, dissatisfied and a 5 year franchise commitment is a long time to hold out if you are unhappy! Equally, if you enjoy knowing what you will be doing on a day to day basis then find a franchise that offers you that level of predictability. Also bear in mind that any business that you run will have a certain degree of sameness in terms of the regular tasks that need doing at regular times – that is one of the joys (or miseries depending on your outlook) of running your own business. Equally, from this perspective, for example, also think about the on-going monthly fees you will need to pay to the franchisor. Would you prefer those fees to be fixed, so you know exactly how much you are paying out every month to the franchisor regardless of your income or would you prefer those costs to be variable, based on the revenues you generate in that month?

Am I a Cool Cucumber or Likely to Get Emotional? We all have different levels of tolerance towards stress, problems and adversity. It is essential to recognise what your likely response is in a crisis so that you can match yourself to the right franchise for you. If you like to live your life by the seat of your pants and respond pretty well to a high pressured environment then an 'emergency response' franchise will suit you well i.e. drain clearing, securing properties after break-ins. If you are more of an emotional responder then choose something that limits your tendency towards a stress response.

Do I Want to Work on My Own or Manage a Team? If you find it difficult or don't like managing others then be wary of franchises that involve you leading a team. Or at the very least ensure that the franchisor's training offers full support to help you overcome that weakness. Managing staff can be one of the biggest problems in a business owner's life. Do you really want that responsibility?

What Am I Interested In? Do you have a passion or interest that you could fulfil whilst running a business? Having your own business is an ideal opportunity for you to do what you love and love what you do. Doing what you are passionate about is a powerful driver. What do you love doing? Swimming, cooking, gardening, teaching, building, networking... list all your interests below because you never know... there may be a franchised business out there that could be right up your street! Jot down all the things that you are interested in or passionate about:

How Much Time Can I Commit to Training? Depending on the complexity of the business, the training programme may be as short as a few days or could be a number of weeks over a period of time. What are your personal circumstances? Can you take the necessary time out to receive the training you require to launch your franchise business?

What Are My Lifestyle Requirements that I Need to Consider? It is important to take the time to look at your life and the commitments you have to ensure that you choose a franchise opportunity that aligns with your life. So for instance:

- What days can I work?

- What hours can I work?
- Do my hours need to revolve around schooling or other personal/family commitments?
- How flexible can my working week be?
- Are there any times during the year when I can't work?
- How many weeks holiday do I want?
- Do I want to work from home or to be based elsewhere?
- If I want to work from home, is there the space for equipment, etc?
- Do I want something local to me or am I prepared to drive?
- Do I have any health problems that have an impact on my capacity to work?
- Do I want some something physical and active?
- What do I find stressful?

How Much Do I Want to Earn? Most people want to invest in a business to bring income into their lives. For some people, the purpose of the franchise may be to generate a second income to fund family perks such as holidays, children's activities and schooling, etc. For others, the purpose of buying a franchise will be to create a full-time income that affords them the lifestyle they aspire to. Be very clear about how much you want to earn and the minimum you would need to earn for the franchise opportunity to be a viable one for you. Also be realistic, a franchise investment fee of £2,500 is unlikely to yield an income of £500,000 per annum! Not only will you need to be realistic about the earnings potential from the franchise but also how quickly you can expect these returns. With some businesses you will be making money within the first month you start trading, with others it may take several months for your business to build momentum and public awareness.

How Much Am I Willing to Invest? It is really important from the outset to know what your maximum budget is and to restrict your searches to opportunities within that budget. Never gamble that which you are not prepared to lose. Ultimately any investment in a business is a gamble – there are no guarantees your business will be successful and that you will make your money back. That being said, be clear about what time period you would ideally like to recoup your investment in, and build your business plan around that. And finally, if there is a specific franchise that you love the look of but don't have the necessary funds – might you be willing to get the backing of a commercial lender to make your dream come true? How far are you prepared to go to make your dreams come true?

Do I Want to Be Tied to Performance Targets? Some franchise operations set minimum performance targets for you to meet on a weekly or monthly basis. For instance, this could be delivering X number of exercise classes per week. If you do not meet those targets then you could be in breach of the Franchise Agreement. Other franchisors allow you the flexibility to set your own pace of work and develop the business as you see fit. Be clear on what basis you want your business to operate. If performance targets motivate you then a business based on such a model may stimulate you.

Do take the time to go through the above questions really thoroughly. I know it is exciting and you want to get out there now and find the business of your dreams. However, the more time you invest in this initial background research and self-awareness exercise the better prepared you will be to find the right franchise for you!

CHAPTER 9

What to do to make a sound franchise investment?

By the time you get to this stage of the process, you will be starting to feel really excited. You've decided that buying a franchise is the right option for you. You've discovered that you have the potential makings of a great franchisee and you are now equipped with detailed information about what type of franchise opportunity might be right for you. You may have narrowed down the vast choice of franchise options to a small shortlist or you may even have your heart firmly set on the 'one'! Either way, you will need to hit the brakes and make sure you go through some crucial activities to ensure that the investment you make in your franchise business is a sound one.

Remember what Clive said in Chapter 2, *"there is nothing to stop a company from offering a franchise regardless of how long they have been trading and how successful they are."* Whilst UK law stipulates that a franchisor cannot give misleading or untrue information to you, the onus is 100% on you to do all the necessary checks to ensure that what you are about to embark on is a sound investment for you. Chapter 4, Buying a Franchise, will have familiarised you with the different stages involved in making a franchise investment. In addition, here are some of the top points to consider as you go through the process of 'due diligence' and explore in detail the franchise offering being presented to you.

Understand the Industry

Take your time to develop an understanding of the franchise industry and the industry you are interested in buying a franchise in. At this time, like no other in the history of mankind, we have a wealth of information at our finger tips. There is no excuse for not knowing! Get on the internet, read newspapers articles, visit your local library, attend a seminar for Prospective Franchisees run by national organisations such as the British Franchise Association, visit franchise shows, seek out organisations such as EWIF (Encouraging Women in Franchising)... all and any of these things will arm you with the background knowledge you need about the franchise industry and more specifically the industry you are thinking of joining.

It is important that you fully understand the context within which you are making your investment. Is it a booming industry or one in decline? What are the challenges that the industry is facing? What is the competition like? What are the trends and projections for the next 5-10 years? This information will give you a background picture about the market and how franchising 'should' work upon which to assess the individual franchise opportunities that you explore.

Do Your Research

Take the time to extensively research the specific franchise operation you are interested in investing in even before you contact the franchisor directly:

- Explore the central website from a customer's perspective – how easy is it to use and find the information you need.
- Be a mystery shopper and visit at least one franchised operation, where possible, to see how it actually works and how it feels to you.
- Download information from Companies House about the company and its directors to see how long they have been trading. Depending on how big the company is you may even be able to download their full accounts. Generally speaking, the longer the business has been in existence the lower the risks as they will have had a longer period of time to test the model they are franchising.
- Download any available information for potential franchisees from the franchisor's website and carefully read the information. Make notes of anything that springs to mind, as you read about the offering, that you would like to find out more about or need clarification for. If the information is not available to download, call the franchisor and request a Franchise Brochure/Prospectus.

Be Clear About Costs

As you now know there will be certain costs involved in buying your franchise – from the initial investment fee to regular ongoing monthly fees for the duration of the franchise. However, you need to be sure that you are clear about all the initial and ongoing costs involved. For instance:

- What is <u>not</u> included in the initial franchise fee that you must account for as part of the business set up costs?
- How much working capital should be included as part of the initial investment?
- What are the on-going monthly fees? Are the fees fixed or variable based on the revenues the business generates?
- What are the costs of renewing the franchise at the end of the initial franchise term?

Double Check Everything

As you continue through the stages of buying a franchise you will be presented with lots of information. It is your responsibility to double check this information and where necessary to find your own evidence to back the franchisor's claims. Doing these double checks will greatly enhance your confidence in the franchise you are considering and enhance your trust in the franchisor. Remember that during this process you have the right to ask as many questions as you want/need, to be satisfied that this the right franchise for you. There are lots of questions you can and should ask your franchisor – you can check some of these out in Chapter 17 – Franchisee Check Lists.

Hire a Specialist Franchise Lawyer

The Franchise Agreement is a legally binding contract. There will be extensive clauses about what you can and cannot do. Unless you have a solid background in law, it is a worthwhile investment retaining the services of a specialist franchising lawyer to examine all the paperwork for you. They have experience of helping thousands of franchisees like you to check the details of such contracts. They will alert you to any terms and conditions that could be problematic for you in the future and make recommendations for amendments to the contract where necessary. A list of specialist Franchise Lawyers can be found on the British Franchise Association website.

Create a Business Plan

Benjamin Franklin once said, *'If you fail to plan, you are planning to fail.'* The success of your franchise business depends on you creating a solid business plan. Whilst it may not be one of the most exciting activities that you will undertake in your franchise career, it is one of the most important. And if you have never written a business plan then don't worry, your franchisor should be prepared to help you in that area. If the franchisor does not have a business plan template that you can use, you can download business plans for free from the franchise section of the High Street banks' websites. The process of writing the business plan will enable you to:

- Analyse your local territory and likely demand for your business
- Understand the local competition and how you are different
- Check the impact of different scenarios on your financial forecasts
- Forecast sales, revenues, cash flow and profits
- Understand how quickly you can expect to make a return on your investment
- Give an overview and a plan of how you expect the business to perform
- Professionally position your business proposition to banks should you require additional finance

Speak with Existing Franchisees

You need to put matters into perspective. The franchisor wants to sell franchises to expand their business and therefore will want to position their business opportunity in the best light possible. I'm not saying that a franchisor would lie but it is in your interest to take the information you receive from a franchisor and do your own checks to ensure that everything stacks up. One of the best ways to do this is to speak to existing franchisees within the network. Your franchisor will probably put you in touch with a few franchisees for you to speak to and in all likelihood they will have been chosen because their business is going well. It is down to you, to go on the franchise website, find other franchisees within the network and contact them directly about their experiences. By speaking to existing franchisees you will gain a more frank and realistic view of what it is like working with the franchisor and running this type of business. Some questions you may choose to ask include:

- What caused you to choose this franchise? What do you enjoy the most about running this business?
- What was your business background and what skills did you have before buying the franchise?
- Are you happy with the revenues your business is generating? Have those revenues met your expectations? Is your business profitable?
- Are you happy with your investment? How long has it taken for you to realise a return on your investment?
- Did the franchisor help you properly estimate the costs? Were there any hidden costs you were not aware of? What were those costs?
- Did you receive adequate training to run the business well? Is there anything that was missing from the training?
- How many hours to you spend every week working 'in' and 'on' the business? How does that fit with your initial expectations of how much time you would be spending

running the business?

- What is your relationship like with the franchisor? How much support have you received from the franchisor?

- What have been the biggest challenges of running the business? Is there anything that has affected your business?

- With what you know now, what would you do differently if you were buying a franchise now? What one piece of advice would you give a potential new franchisee like me?

Check the Connection

A franchise agreement is a partnership based on a legal relationship. The relationship between you and the franchisor is perhaps the most important aspect of the business – relying on both parties for it to succeed. If you don't 'connect' with the franchisor now then you are unlikely to get on in the future once the pressures of running the business come into play.

It is important that you both feel good about working with one another after all you want to feel comfortable sharing your fears, worries, mistakes and problems as well as your successes with your franchisor. When you ask the franchisor questions, check how eager and open they are in answering them. If the connection is not there then this may not be an appropriate franchise investment for you.

Be Honest

I know you want the franchisor to want <u>you</u> however, it is important that you complete the Franchise Application Form and conduct yourself in the Franchise Interview as honestly as possible. Just as much as you want the franchisor to be honest with you about the opportunity on offer, the franchisor needs you to be honest about your skills, background, ambitions, etc.

For this franchising partnership to work then the foundations must be built on mutual honesty and trust! If you are right for the franchise, then it will be in the franchisor's interests to help you fill any gaps/weaknesses you may have.

Be Objective

When you go through the process of buying a business it can be very easy to get carried away with the dream... after all it's so close you can practically touch it! For you to minimise the risk of making an unsound investment it's important that you remain objective and realistic and do your due diligence thoroughly. Look at the deal on offer very carefully – does everything stack up and make sense? Could you get a better deal elsewhere? Do the costs match your expectations of what you will receive from the franchisor in return? And finally, if the deal looks too good to be true then it probably is! Walk away.

Trust Your Intuition

You have 6 senses in total – sight, sound, touch, taste, smell and intuition. Your intuition is a very powerful resource... it is the perceptive insight you have to experience a feeling of inner knowing that cannot be logically explained. And I know that you have experienced that many times in the past. Please trust your intuition – if something doesn't feel right then don't fight it, accept it. Your sixth sense is as reliable as any of your other senses if you tune in to it. It may not always be the logical choice but your intuition is your unconscious mind speaking to you – you'd be well advised to listen to it. And of course the more you listen, the louder it will speak to you. When I was interviewing the wonderful women for the case studies in Part 3, I was amazed at how much their sense of intuition came into play when making their franchise investment decision. Some even called the whole experience 'fate'!

CHAPTER 10

Summary

Many people love the idea of being their own boss and running their own business but the truth is that it's hard work and it's not for everyone. The process can be made a little easier by investing in a franchised business model but still not everyone is suited to running that type of business. And perhaps you have recognised that franchising is not for you in which case buying this book will have been a very worthwhile investment saving you a lot of money and stress in the long run.

However, you may be one of the many people for whom franchising is a perfect fit. If this is the case, you will improve your chances of finding that perfect franchise match by taking the time to reflect on who you are, your skills, desires and needs. Armed with that information you can confidently begin to sift through the hundreds of different franchise opportunities that are open to you and once you have narrowed your choice down to a handful then please follow the guidance in Chapters 4, 9 and Part 4, to help you with the due diligence process you must undertake to make sure you make a sound investment.

With so many different types of business start-up options and franchises available to you please make sure you are very clear about your motivation. You owe it to yourself to use the opportunity to run your own business as a way to achieve a fulfilling life. If you chase the money rather than your passion you may end up regretting it. Do what you love and the rewards will follow!

As you dive into your dream of self-employment and franchise business ownership please remember that this is your life and you are responsible for it. To make it the life you want you have to take action. Running your own business is never easy but it can be massively rewarding and fun. As a franchisee you will be given a formula for potential success but ultimately the success of your business is not down to what franchise you buy or the economic climate or any other factor other than you. The success of your business lies firmly in your own hands. The key to your business success is very simply – YOU! And you are a formidable force – stronger, more resourceful and courageous than you can ever imagine. So, allow yourself to explore what type of business could bring you the greatest level of personal fulfillment, do your research, believe in yourself and make it happen!

PART 3

FRANCHISEE CASE STUDIES

CHAPTER 11

Recognition Express
by Sally Findlay

Sally Findlay is the owner of the Recognition Express franchise in Mid-Surrey, which provides tailored branded merchandise solutions for local businesses. She bought the franchise in 2004 after wanting a new direction after working as a Senior Project Manager in the City.

"I wanted to go back to working for a smaller company but had outgrown that sort of job. I was looking for ideas and not sure what direction to take."

Whilst Sally came to the realisation that she wanted to work for herself, she didn't have *'a genius idea'* to form the foundations of a business of her own. A friend who owned a kitchen renewal franchise suggested that buying a franchise might be the perfect solution.

Intrigued by the possibilities, but without any specific idea of what she wanted, Sally went to a franchise exhibition at the NEC, Birmingham in September 2003 to explore and find out more.

"Buying a franchise is such a good idea. You can use someone else's tried and tested business idea."

From her visit to the NEC and information from the British Franchise Association guide, Sally quickly realised the vast choice of franchises that were available to buy. She found that some franchise opportunities were better than others in terms of what they offered and the level of investment they required.

"Some franchisors based their fees on turnover or profit whilst others charged regular fixed fees. I decided that a franchisor who charged fees on profit/turnover would have a vested interest in the franchisee's business doing well."

Having done her research and with a completely open mind as to what she might invest in, Sally ended up making her choice based on very practical things like working hours, projected earnings, the ability to work from home to start with and the initial investment cost. She finally narrowed her selection down to 8 franchises and expected to commit within the next 5 years. However, when major changes took place at work, she found herself in a position to either find another job or take the plunge into franchising. Sally didn't need a better *'sign'* than that. By April 2004, Sally had signed the Franchise Agreement with Recognition Express and was the proud owner of her own business.

Sally naturally had some doubts and concerns. What if she signed up with *'someone questionable that would take her money and run?'* What if she *'wouldn't be any good at running her own business?'* She had never been self-employed and no one else in her family had ever run a business so she had no ready access to support. Indeed, all her family were successful professionals, high up in their fields and she worried that she might fail in such a venture.

"But that's why I chose to buy a franchise. It's much safer. You are statistically less likely to go bust than starting up your own business from scratch."

The first year or so was *'full-on'* for Sally. She worked all day, every day. She admits to getting completely wrapped up in her business – visiting customers, answering quotes, creating designs, doing accounts, marketing, phoning new prospects, ordering stock, dealing with suppliers, checking production... And what Sally hadn't realised was that even with the support and training from the franchisor, it took time to learn everything about the business. Things quickly settled down though and now Sally works about 45 hours per week and has a complement of staff to support her. In hindsight, Sally wishes she had been more ambitious and taken more risks early on in the business. But ultimately she says, *"I have a very solid business with a strong customer base."*

So what advice would Sally give women considering buying a franchise?

"It's much easier to buy a Franchise than you think but choose carefully. Pick a franchisor with a really good reputation. Do your research. Be clear about what you want and open to what is out there. And once you have bought the Franchise, listen to your franchisor. They really do know better than you!"

CHAPTER 12

Just Shutters

by Sarah Gale

Sarah Gale became the first female Just Shutters franchisee in April 2012. Just Shutters are a small but growing business supplying and fitting plantation shutters. Sarah's move into the world of shutters was a good personal fit based on her previous background, experience and knowledge as a journalist and PR specialising in interiors. However, what Sarah hadn't considered when she set up her PR business in 2009 was the impact of working 'for herself by herself'. Whilst she was very happy running and administering her PR business she really missed not being part of a team. What therefore appealed to Sarah about buying a franchise was that you would be running a business 'for yourself' but not 'by yourself'.

"I wanted a different direction for my career after running my own business for around two years, with the chance to interact with more people. When I saw the Just Shutters franchise opportunity I thought 'That looks really interesting'."

And what was of particular interest to Sarah about Just Shutters was that it was not gender specific.

"Quite a lot of franchises targeting women were meant to be run on a part-time basis. That would suit some women but I had reached a stage in my life where I wanted to ramp up my work and earn proper money – on a full-time basis whilst still being able to fit it around my family dynamics."

Sarah did have a number of concerns though about her investment in the shutter business. Firstly, there was the technical side of the business. Whilst from the outset, Sarah had no intention of being the one fitting shutters forever, she realised that in the early days of the business she would have to. She worried that her lack of DIY experience and skills would hold her back. However, Chris, the owner, reassured her that he would support her on installations until she was up to the required standard. Sarah admits that she wasn't the quickest learner and that it took time to work through some of the issues around her practical training and skills, however within a few months these had been addressed. The other concern she had was her lack of formal sales training. However, with her husband having always been in sales she knew she could count on him to support her in that area. Indeed, Sarah believes that:

"Support from your partner is important when buying a

franchise. They know you and can help you identify what you would be well suited to. It's good to have someone supporting you, who can help you if you need it and who is enthusiastic about what you are doing."

The process of becoming a Just Shutters franchisee was a relatively swift one for Sarah. She first enquired about their offering in January 2012 and arranged to meet with the owners of the business at the Franchise Show in February. Sarah's connection and relationship with the franchisor was an important deciding factor and when she met the owners her interest in buying their franchise was strongly reinforced. She proceeded to carry out the necessary due diligence: attending an 'experience day', speaking to other franchisees, looking into the trading history of Just Shutters and putting together a business plan of her own. The business plan, Sarah explains, is *"really worth doing to distil your thoughts"*. Finally, having received advice from a Franchise Advisor and also a lawyer specialising in franchising, and with all her concerns put to rest, Sarah signed the franchise agreement in April 2012 and launched her Just Shutters franchise at an exhibition the following month.

Sarah's intention from the outset was to work on the business full-time. She spends on average 45-50 hours per week working 'in' and 'on' her business. Every week is different, split between a range of activities including appointments, measurements, fittings, exhibiting at shows, marketing and general business administration. She says she is really happy with her decision and now has the best of both worlds – her own, growing business and the extended team/support she longed for.

So what advice would Sarah give women considering buying a franchise?

"It's important to seek out answers and keep asking questions until you are fully satisfied. At the beginning, I didn't know the questions to ask because I didn't understand the technical side. I should have spent more time considering that and speaking to fitters in more depth. That being said, I have really increased my problem solving skills and I am proud to own a thriving local business with strong prospects for the future."

Looking for a business that works around you?

This proven pre-school children's franchise could be music to your ears!

- No experience necessary
- Flexible working hours
- Set your own targets
- Low start up costs – high returns
- Full training and ongoing support
- Fully prepared lesson structure
- Developed and run by Child Professionals
- Music professionally recorded

Opportunities available across the UK.

Musical Minis

business made fun!

To request an information pack:-

visit: www.musicalminis.co.uk

call us on: **020 8868 0001**

or e-mail us at: enquiries@musicalminis.co.uk

CHAPTER 13

Musical Minis
by Leena Thakker

Leena Thakker bought the Oxfordshire Musical Minis (music classes for preschoolers from birth – 4 years) franchise in February 2009. Leena's background is in Sales, Marketing and Business Development. When she was pregnant with her eldest daughter, she worked as an International Business Development Manager which required extensive foreign travel. As her pregnancy progressed the job became increasingly untenable and she soon realised that she would have to think of other options. Following the birth of her daughter, she set up a marketing consultancy business which worked really well and grew very quickly. It too involved lots of travel and soon enough, prompted by a second pregnancy, she found herself in a position where she wasn't able to manage the workload. She decided to put her business on hold and look at other possibilities that would be more family friendly.

Franchising really appealed to Leena - offering a recognised brand with a proven formula for success. In particular, Leena was keen to choose a franchise with a relatively low capital investment, where all the costs were included in the franchise fee and that had the potential for repeat business. Leena loves children so the franchising opportunities she considered were all child related.

"Parents will spend money on their children and will cut back elsewhere. Also the children's market is always going to be unsaturated and if a business provides the right type of product or service, there is no reason why it won't succeed. The economy and recession has not had any impact on my business whatsoever."

Musical Minis in particular had first captured her attention, when she had taken Anya, her first born to local classes. This interest was rekindled when she started taking her second daughter to classes too. It was at this time, November 2008 that she saw a Musical Minis newsletter advertising the sale of the Oxfordshire franchise.

"That's how it really started. The right opportunity came at the right time. I knew the format having taken both my children there so I felt this gave me a head start. In addition, I found that the Musical Minis programme is very well structured and it really helped both my girls' development in their Early Years, in key areas such as speech, co-ordination and development of their social and interpersonal skills."

Leena's only concerns about buying the franchise were whether she would be able to make it work and how long it would take to recoup her initial investment. What she hadn't anticipated was how quickly the business would grow. Her intention was to run the business on a very part-time basis – just a couple of sessions a week until her youngest started school. However, demand was incredible and within the first term she was running 6 classes per week. The success of her classes meant that within 1 year of purchasing the franchise she had recouped the initial investment.

"I had bought the franchise when Alaina, my youngest daughter was 2. This meant that I could take her to classes with me, without the cost of childcare. Alaina was a very good toddler and so I was able to run the classes successfully. However, like every parent, the guilt of not spending enough time with your children soon crept in. However, I convinced myself that this was why I was doing what I was doing – to have a business that gave me the flexibility and autonomy without worrying about childcare costs, school holidays etc. A business that really fitted in with my family life."

Leena described her working week as 'hectic'! Her franchise now delivers 21 classes every week along with additional Musical Minis parties at weekends. Leena personally runs 13 of the classes and as she is not local to her franchise area, she admits to spending a lot of time travelling. As her classes increase so does the administration. Her day usually starts at 5am and ends sometime after midnight to enable her to fit all her work and family commitments. She admits that there is no requirement from Musical Minis Head Office for her to work so hard. Indeed, that was one of the factors that appealed to her about investing in this specific franchise.

"I know I put undue pressure on myself, as I am very ambitious. But this is my choice. There is no pressure or demands from Head Office to deliver a certain number of classes a week. In fact, Some franchisees only run 5 classes per week and are happy with that. I've chosen to continue growing my business."

With a rapidly growing business, Leena has found herself needing extra staff support. And this is where Leena has experienced real challenges with her business. Indeed, one of her Leaders ran the classes so ineffectively which resulted in some of her classes being closed down.

"Taking on staff opens up a whole new area to the business. After having some staffing problems, I have learnt to do things differently now. I take on someone as an Assistant to work alongside me for a period of time. In conjunction with their 'on-the-job' training they also start to receive formal training to become a Leader. I then carry out an

assessment whereby they have to run one of my classes. On completion of the assessment successfully they start running classes, whilst I still attend the classes for a few weeks, before letting them take over on their own. This seems to have worked well, even though the whole process takes a lot longer. But at least I then know that my classes are being run exactly how I want them to be conducted."

So what advice would Leena give women considering buying a franchise?

"I would recommend that potential franchisees look out for any hidden costs and what is involved in running the business. The Musical Minis Franchise had no additional training or support costs, whereas a lot of franchises have additional costs attached. Purchasing the Musical Minis Franchise meant that after my training (inclusive in the Franchise fee) I had everything I needed to get my business started. It is also really important to meet with and get on with the franchisor. Although we are pretty autonomous, it is a Franchise and at the end of the day it is the reputation of the company which is important. Also, by meeting the franchisor, you will get a good feeling about them as people, their branding and really if it is the right business for you. Finally, make sure you know the reason why you are buying the Franchise. My reasons were to find a business which offered me the flexibility. Admittedly, the

business has grown much faster than I had anticipated which has meant that family sacrifices have been made but having said that my business offers me and my family the lifestyle we love. For me it has been the right decision to purchase a Franchise and for Women who are looking for a career change for whatever reason, I would definitely recommend exploring the opportunities of purchasing a franchise."

CHAPTER 14

Water Babies
by Kate Evans

Kate Evans owns the Cornwall & South Devon Water Babies franchise. She bought it in December 2009 but in many respects the wheels of destiny were set in motion 5 years ago when she first attended a local Water Babies class with her daughter, Polly. At that time she was so taken by the concept and delivery of Water Babies classes that she even considered the idea of becoming a teacher. As Kate's family grew, her career as an A&E doctor became more difficult to juggle with family life. She began wondering about the alternatives. But Kate did not have any business experience and realised from the outset that whatever she did she would need support. As a doctor, she knew she wanted to do something she believed in, was worthwhile, gave her satisfaction but also ticked the 'family friendly' box.

"Water Babies is so family friendly. I love the job. I love the teaching. It's great fun. We really believe in what we do and the support I get from Head Office is beyond anything I could have imagined."

It was whilst on maternity leave with her second child, that the idea of running a Water Babies franchise started to crystallise in her mind. Kate decided to contact her local Water Babies franchisee and ask her advice about running a franchise. She secretly thought, *'Wouldn't it be perfect if my local Water Babies franchisee wanted to sell her business'*. Stroke of luck or destiny? As it happened her local Water Babies franchisee did indeed want to sell her business as a going concern. Kate was already sure that she wanted to run a Water Babies franchise and consequently needed no further convincing. Yes she had concerns, after all she had no business experience and she was going to leave a very secure job with a stable income and she worried that in the 1st year, due to the steep learning curve of running your own business, she might see her children even less than before.

"It was a big investment and a big risk. I even took my name off the register of doctors. I don't regret it though. It was the best decision of my life."

The process, after having spoken with the local franchisee and the Water Babies co-founder in early 2009 was straight forward but fairly protracted. Kate went on a British Franchise Association one day course for people thinking about buying a franchise. Kate found it really useful to get an impartial insight into the industry and tips as to what to look out for when considering buying a franchise. She then submitted an application form to Water Babies and spent a day at their Head Office.

"It wasn't really an interview – it was more of an opportunity for both parties to find out more about each other. A two-way process to see if we were compatible."

After that there was all the paperwork side of the business to go through – developing the business plan, growth plans, examining financial forecasts, looking at the existing franchisees plans. All in all that took from around May to September 2009. Once all the due diligence work had been completed, Kate went on the Water Babies Teacher Training course and in the October started teaching some of the classes she was about to take over. Finally in December 2009, everything was signed off.

Three years on, one of the things Kate loves most about running her own franchise is that it is so varied. No two weeks are the same. She typically works 3 days (20-24 hours) per week (short days that fit around the school run) – be it in the office, out marketing, speaking to mums or teaching lessons.

"I don't work as many hours as I probably should. I'm lucky as my husband has a good job and we have a fulltime administrator and 6 teachers working in the business. I balance work and home life and often base decisions on family needs rather than business needs."

So what advice would Kate give women considering buying a franchise?

"Do your homework and research. Really look into the franchisor, talk to existing franchisees (and not just the ones Head Office recommends) and make sure you factor everything into your business plan. Be prepared for a steep learning curve and be clear about your reasons for buying the franchise. And finally, after all the research and questions.... just go for it and have fun."

"Owning a Signs Express franchise has been the best move I've made."

Mark Kendall - Signs Express, Southampton

"I have pride and satisfaction as my own boss with the added benefit of being part of a national brand. Through training and support I am able to focus on growing my business and have the flexibility to spend time with my family and enjoy life!"

Signs are our business, make them yours.
Call 0800 731 2255 or visit www.signsexpress.co.uk/franchise

bfa

Investment level
£120,000 + VAT

SIGNS EXPRESS

CHAPTER 15

Signs Express
by Anne Hitch

Anne Hitch originally bought the Peterborough & Kings Lynn Signs Express franchise with her husband in 2001. Signs Express is the UK & Ireland's leading signs and graphics franchise.

Anne was very much attracted to the idea of going into business and working for herself. However, whilst she had recently completed a business degree, Anne had no previous experience of running her own business. What she really liked about the idea of investing in a franchise was the back-up, support and technical advice offered as part of the package.

"You are working for yourself but you are not on your own."

Her entry into the world of franchising came via a friend who owned a Signs Express franchise, whom she helped with his accounts and administration for 6 months. It was at that time that she found out about the opportunity to buy the Peterborough & Kings Lynn franchise. She made her initial enquiry to the Signs Express Head Office in October 2000 and the deal was signed off in March 2001. Having already worked in a Signs Express franchise meant that she had considerable knowledge of the business and its systems so was able to *'hit the ground running'*.

At the beginning, it was convenient for her to work part-time and for her husband to work in the business on a full-time basis. Slowly but surely her input and hours increased until her partner moved to *'pastures new'*. Anne took full responsibility for the running of the business – becoming the only sole woman running a Signs Express franchise across a network of over 70 franchisees. Anne doesn't understand why more women don't sign up as Signs Express franchisees, or in similar types of franchises, as she believes the business is perfectly suited to women's skills.

> *"In essence it's a management franchise. Everything we do is logical and sequential."*

Anne believes that women have a massive skills set that they don't themselves recognise but that in business really sets them apart. Although Anne's husband had a background in engineering, Anne had done a lot of practical things in her past which seemed to all fit perfectly together for the Signs Express opportunity. She describes it as feeling like:

> *"Like every road you have ever travelled before has led you here."*

On a more personal level, for Anne, becoming a franchisee was a complete change for her.

"It's a lifestyle change. I work long hours but I organise my hours to suit myself. The main difference is that the responsibility is all yours. It's no one else's. You can't just walk away."

In particular came the sense of responsibility of knowing she was committing herself to a Franchise Agreement and a considerable bank loan. If things didn't go according to plan then essentially her home would be at risk. She also wondered whether working with her husband would work.

"Just because you are in a relationship with someone doesn't mean you can work well together."

Although on most days Anne start work at 7.30am and ends at about 5.30pm, every day is different though within that - a changing cocktail of managing her team of 6 staff, quoting for jobs, dealing with suppliers, overseeing accounts, monitoring sales activities, engaging in marketing and going out to visit clients. It's hard work but for Anne it is all worthwhile – she is building something solid for her future and continues to invest heavily in the growth of the business.

So what advice would Anne give women considering buying a franchise?

"A certain amount of realism is required. You have to put a lot of hours and effort in. Don't expect a quick return. It's a long-term return. For women it's important to have confidence in your own skills and what you can bring to the business. Women have great foresight and instinct. Be a woman in business and don't try to be a man. Be true to yourself and work it to your advantage."

CHAPTER 16

Care2U
by Laura Macrae

Laura Macrae purchased the Cafe2U Aberdeen West franchise in June 2009. Cafe2U is a mobile coffee franchise system, delivering coffee and food to businesses, events and functions.

It had always been Laura's dream to run her own coffee shop. It was only when a Cafe2U van started delivering to her husband's workplace that Laura realised that her dream could become a reality.

"I knew about franchising but what I didn't realise was that a lot of the brands you see on the high street are actually franchise businesses."

Around February 2009, her husband got chatting with the local Cafe2U franchisee who told him that she was wanted to sell her business. Laura didn't need to look much further. She knew there was nothing else like it in her area and the thought of being part of a franchise network with support at the end of the phone really appealed to her. She loved the

Cafe2U concept and this was the ideal opportunity for her to do something she was passionate about and loved. Her main dilemma was whether she should invest in a brand new Cafe2U franchise or buy the existing one on offer. In the end, Laura decided to buy the existing Aberdeen West franchise.

"The deal was too good to resist. The lady selling the franchise needed to get rid of it quickly because of personal circumstances. Buying this was way significantly cheaper than me buying a new Cafe2U franchise. I suppose I was in the right place at the right time!"

Clearly, running a mobile coffee business was different to her original dream of owning a coffee shop but with the recession biting deep and companies closing, it made absolute sense. The concept of the mobile coffee van meant that if a company closed, she could go elsewhere.

"You are not reliant on business coming to you. You are free to go to where the business is which even means you can take the business to events at weekends such as school fetes, charity events and even the Highland Games."

Laura had been a successful Account Manager for an off-shore survival training company prior to taking the plunge and buying her franchise. Her job had been well paid but ultimately she wasn't enjoying what she was doing anymore. Whilst going from secure, well paid employment to self-employment worried Laura, she knew she had to do it for the sake of her health and sanity. Other than that, having only ever previously driven cars, Laura's only other concern about buying the franchise centered around driving the Cafe2U van. This quickly dissipated and now she prides herself in being able to squeeze the van into the tiniest of spaces. What Laura loves about her new life is that she has 100% flexibility and she can be home in the afternoons in time for when her daughter gets back from school. She has a very loyal customer base, loves what she does and is now thinking of the future and the possibility of expanding her business further.

So what advice would Laura give women considering buying a franchise?

"Look at the proposition as a whole picture as well as the small print. Remember that when you are self-employed there are always other things to do. That can make it hard to switch off. Also make sure you have the full support and backing of your family. To me that was really important and I was lucky to have my husband's support from the outset."

PART 4

USEFUL INFORMATION

CHAPTER 17

Franchisee check lists

The British Franchise Association
– 50 Questions to Ask a Franchisor

Here are 50 questions that we recommend you put to any franchise business that you are considering joining. All reputable franchisors will welcome these questions and indeed some of them will insist that you follow certain steps in the journey to becoming a franchisee —including, for example, that you take legal advice before signing the franchise agreement. You should never be afraid to ask a question and should carefully note and weigh up the reply making sure you receive a proper response. You should not rush your decisions when considering franchise opportunities.

On their Business
1. How long have you been in franchising?
2. How many franchised businesses are you running at the moment?
3. What are the addresses of these businesses?
4. May I interview any number of these franchisees? And may I choose whom I interview?
5. What does your head office organisation consist of?

6. Can you demonstrate your capacity to provide the necessary follow-up services?
7. May I take up your bank reference?
8. Are there any other referees whom I may approach?
9. How many franchise business failures have been experienced by your franchisees?
10. On what basis do you choose your franchisees — how selective are you?

On Costs

11. How much does your franchise opportunity cost, what does this price include and what capital costs will be incurred in addition to this price? And what for?
12. How much working capital do I need?
13. What will be the gross profit margin and what costs will I incur in arriving at a net profit? (Do these figures take my salary and depreciation into account?)
14. May I see actual accounts which confirm or fail to confirm your projections?
15. Did you run your own pilot schemes before franchising?
16. If not, why not?
17. Whether you did or not, what is the extent of your own cash investment in the business?
18. What financing arrangements can you make and what terms for repayment will there be? What rate of interest will be required — and will the finance company want security?

On Methods

19. Is the franchise business seasonal?

20. When is the best time to open?

21. What fees do you charge?

22. Do you take any commission on supplies of goods or materials to a franchisee? Do I have to purchase all or just scheduled items from you? Does this apply to equipment?

23. Will I be obliged to maintain a minimum fee or minimum purchase of goods? What happens if I fail to meet this commitment?

24. What advertising and promotional expenditure do you incur?

25. Do I have to contribute to it, if so how much?

26. What initial services do you offer?

27. Do you train me? Who pays for my training? Where do I go for training?

28. What continuing services do you provide after the franchise business has commenced?

29. May I have a copy of your franchise contracts?

30. Does this contract permit me to sell my business? What restrictions are there affecting my rights to sell the business?

31. For how long is the franchise granted?

32. What happens at the end of that period?

On Your Involvement

33. What will happen if I do not like the franchise business? Upon what basis can I terminate the contract?

34. Who will be my link with you after I have opened for business?

Can I meet some of your staff?

35. What point of sale and promotional literature do you supply and what do I have to pay for it?

36. What will be the opening hours of the franchise business?

37. Will I own the equipment necessary to operate the business when I have cleared the finance company?

38. How soon will I have to spend money on redecorating the business premises?

39. How soon will I have to spend money on replacing equipment?

40. Will you find me a site or do I have to find it?

On Communications & Operations

41. What systems do you have for keeping franchisees in touch with you and each other? Do you publish a newsletter? Do you hold seminars?

42. What help will I receive in local advertising and promotion?

43. What exclusive rights do I get?

44. How will I cope with my book-keeping?

45. What can I sell and what can I not sell?

46. Do you provide instruction and operation manuals?

47. What would happen if you misjudged the site and it did not produce the anticipated figures but resulted in a loss?

48. What would happen if I ran into operational problems I was not able to solve? What help would I get?

49. How can I be sure you will do what you promise?

50. Is your company a member of the bfa? If not may we know the reason?

The value of the answers received will be a matter for your judgment. You can, of course, verify the value of the answers by the experience of existing franchisees. Speaking to existing franchisees will form a very important part of your research. They have, after all, been living with the business and with the franchisor for some time already so their responses will help in your decision making. You must choose those whom you wish to interview, you should not let the franchisor feed to you only his best franchisees.

Source:

www.thebfa.org/join-a-franchise/50-questions-to-ask-a-franchisor
(Jan 2013)

Lloyds TSB
– 30 Key Questions About Franchising

Common sense will take you a long way in deciding whether the franchise you are considering will prove right for you. We've prepared the following questions to help you evaluate a franchise before deciding whether to invest. Please bear in mind that this list is for your guidance only and it is not exhaustive. You'll still need to rely on your own judgement before investing in a particular franchise.

The Franchise

1. How long have you been franchising? – Think about their track record and the director's background

2. What professional support have you had in developing your franchise? – Have they used bfa affiliated consultants and lawyers?

3. What is your financial strength? – Ask for last 3 years financial accounts. What capital have they invested and is the business profitable? Is the business financially sound?

4. Who is the main competition? – Is the market developing? How competitive is it? Does the franchise have a competitive advantage or unique selling points? What market research did they do?

5. How many franchisees are there? – Speak to as many as you can as a part of your research

6. What are your development plans? – Are there sufficient resources? How will they impact on your business?

7. How is your Head Office organised? – Management, accounting, sales support, administration. Is this a well organised and significant business?

8. Did you carry out any pilot operations? – If it's a new franchise ask them to demonstrate its success

9. How many franchisees have failed? – What lessons have they learned? Are they prepared to discuss these openly with you?

10. How do you choose your franchisees? – What skills and attributes are they looking for and how selective are they?

11. Are you a member of the British Franchise Association? – If not why?

12. Can I take up references? – Bank reference or other reliable sources

Costs and projections

13. How much does the franchise cost in total? – What is included in the package and how much working capital will be required? Is there any additional expenditure? Is it value for money?

14. What are the ongoing charges? – Management service fee, mark up on goods or services, advertising levy, any other costs?

15. What are the key financial ratios? – Gross profit margin, typical overheads, projected net profit, stock turnover,

debtor days and break-even figure. Are they realistic?

16. Can I see actual trading figures from existing franchisees? – Do these confirm that your projections are achievable?

17. Are there any financial arrangements I should know about? – Vehicle and equipment leasing, supplier terms, national accounts, requirements to replace equipment or refurbish premises

18. Is there a minimum performance requirement? – What happens if you don't achieve it? Is it achievable?

Methods

19. Is the business seasonal? – When is the best time of the year to start trading?

20. Can I choose alternative suppliers? – Am I obliged to buy goods from your nominated suppliers? Are there minimum order levels?

21. Do you allocate exclusive territories? – How many potential customers do you have in your area? How big is your territory? Does the proposed area suit you? What restrictions are there?

22. For how long is the initial franchise licence granted? – Is it renewable? Is there a fee payable on renewal? What happens at the end of the term?

23. What restrictions will there be when I sell the business? – What penalties are there if you terminate the agreement? Are these terms acceptable?

24. What marketing programme do you have? — What are your and the franchisors obligations?

Support

25. What training is provided? — Consider both initial and continuing training. Who pays for it? Is it classroom or field based training?

26. What support do you provide prior to the business launch? — Will you get help with site selection, lease negotiation, design, refurbishment, equipment, vehicles, staff recruitment and stock? What launch support can you expect?

27. What ongoing support do you provide? — Who will be you main point of contact? Are there regular review meetings and field visits?

28. What support is available if you run into difficulties? — Has the franchisor past experience of successfully supporting other franchisees with problems?

29. How often does the network get together? — Are there regular meetings and conferences where you can share best practices and get advice from other franchisees?

30. Can I meet your Head Office team? — What experience do they have and will they be able to support you to grow your business?

Franchising – You Decide

Of course, franchising is not right for everyone. For people who value independence or want to run a business without restrictions or to re-invent the wheel, franchising might not be the right option. Anyone considering investing in a franchise must be prepared to ask some probing questions of the franchisor. Their responses will assist you in deciding whether the franchise is right for you.

If they only seem interested in taking your money and not supporting you develop your own business you should be prepared to walk away. You must be one hundred percent comfortable with the proposed investment. You are looking for a franchisor that is passionate about supporting you to build a successful franchised business which will be beneficial to both parties.

The franchise relationship must be built based upon mutual trust and respect. The franchisor provides support and motivation to their network of franchisees and in turn benefits from their ultimate success through a share of the profits. Running your own business requires self-motivation, stamina and you'll also need the ability to stick at it in adversity. At the same time, you must be prepared to accept the franchisor's rules for their business system. Be honest – Will franchising be right for you?

Ask yourself the following

- Are your goals realistic and attainable?
- Do you have the drive, tenacity and self-discipline to succeed?
- Can you develop and sustain relationships with a wide range of people?
- Do you have the full support of your family?
- Is the price right and will it deliver the returns you need?
- Are you up for the challenge?

The above information has been created and supplied by Lloyds TSB:

http://businesshelp.lloydstsbbusiness.com/industry-focus/franchising/news/ (Jan 2013)

NatWest
– Things to consider

Here are a few pointers to consider when becoming a franchisee:

Price/Set-Up Costs

The start-up costs of a franchise you run from home will be very different from a franchise that needs premises and stock.

To assess your price range, a very rough rule of thumb is to add up your savings and multiply by three. So if you have savings of £20,000, you could expect to be able to finance a franchise with start-up costs of around £60,000.

Many franchisees make the mistake of over-borrowing. This could cause difficulties, particularly in periods of depressed sales or high interest rates.

Running your own business – franchise or otherwise – can be extremely rewarding. It can also be very stressful. You're responsible for your own income, and you may have to invest your life savings or take out a loan against the security of your home. These are serious factors to consider. Just make sure you're going into franchising with your eyes properly open.

Type of Business

This is largely a matter of common sense. Choose a business you'll be happy to work in day-after-day, preferably one where you have some aptitude or affinity and perhaps even some experience.

Here are some points to consider in assessing the best type of business for you:

- Is the franchise serving an established market, or has that market yet to be developed?
- Is the market expanding or declining?
- Is it seasonal?
- Does it depend on trading from highly-specialised sites?
- How strong is the competition?
- Is the franchise competitive in its market?
- What share of the market does it hold?

Once you know your budget and the type of business you're interested in, you have to choose your franchisor. If there are only one or two franchisors in your category, it would be wise to select a second category to avoid having too small a choice. This will also give you a wider selection of territories as many franchise agreements stipulate a geographic territory which the franchisee can operate in.

Check Out the Franchisor

Deciding which franchisor is right for you is the last stage of your assessment process and the most important. You may be right for franchising and the market you have chosen may be full of promise, but this will not make up for an ineffective franchisor.

Think about the following questions:

- Has the franchise been sufficiently tested and are its franchisees successful?
- Do the initial and ongoing fees represent good value for money?
- Do the on-going fees still leave the product or service competitive and provide enough profit to make the business worthwhile?
- Does the franchisor have sufficient financial and management resources to provide the support promised?
- Is the franchisor fair and ethical in all business dealings?
- Is the franchisor a member of the British Franchise Association and abide by their code of practice?
- In the event of the franchisor's failure are there alternative suppliers?

Ending the Agreement

There may be restrictions imposed on you if you decide to leave the franchise. You are unlikely to be allowed to carry on trading under your own name in the same type of business from the same premises.

The above information has been created and supplied by NatWest:

http://www.natwest.com/business/services/market-expertise/franchising/franchisees.ashx#tabs=section1 (Jan 2013)

HSBC

– Top Ten Tips

- Find out what franchises are available by viewing whichfranchise.com – there are also exhibitions, directories and magazines all devoted to franchising.
- Take as much advice as possible – from the bfa, banks, lawyers, accountants, Business Links etc.
- Examine your strengths and weaknesses – what skills do you have? Does the franchisor provide training and back-up to help you overcome any skill gaps?
- Check the franchise is right for you – is the business one you can see yourself running?
- Talk to existing franchisees – what problems did they face, how successful are they?
- Investigate the franchisor – it is important that the franchisor has the financial resources to support a franchise network.
- Examine the marketplace – is there a market for your chosen franchise's goods/services? Is the franchise operating in a market subject to the economic environment?
- Take care with new franchises – has the franchise been piloted, how long has the franchisor been in business?
- Check the legal agreement – has the franchise agreement been vetted by a franchise specialist solicitor?
- Take your time – however enthusiastic you are, don't be rushed and do your homework

The above information has been created and supplied by HSBC:

http://www.business.hsbc.co.uk/1/2/franchising/buying-franchise

(Jan 2013)

CHAPTER 18

Franchise industry sectors

Listed below are a selection of industries that have franchise opportunities. The list is not exhaustive but illustrates the wide range of sectors that operate franchises in the UK:

Accountancy & Financial Franchises

Automotive Franchises

Business to Business Franchises

Business Consulting Franchises

Business Training Franchises

Care & Elderly Franchises

Children Franchises

Cleaning Franchises

Coffee Franchises

Commercial & Industrial Franchises

Communication Franchises

Computer Franchises

Courier Franchises

Delivery & Haulage Franchises

Education Franchises

Estate Agency Franchises

Fitness Franchises

Food & Catering Franchises

Gardening Franchises

Health & Beauty Franchises

High Street Retail Franchises

Home Care Franchises

Home Improvement Franchises

Home Services Franchises

Internet Franchises

Lawn Care Franchises

Letting Agency Franchises

Magazine Franchises

Merchandising Franchises

Mortgage Franchises

Motoring Franchises

Pest Control Franchises

Pet Franchises

Photography Franchises

Printing & Sign Franchises

Professional Services

Property Maintenance & Repair Franchises

Recruitment Franchises

Retail Franchises

Safety & Security Franchises

Sports Franchises

Travel & Leisure Franchises

Vending Franchises

CHAPTER 19

Franchise glossary of terms

BFA

The British Franchise Association was established in 1978 with the aim of regulating franchising on an ethical basis, by granting membership to those franchisors that it considers, meets the demands of its Codes of Ethics and procedures.

Business Format

The term used to describe a franchise where the franchisee buys into the total system of the brand, including the brand name, know-how, training, methodology, systems, procedures and ongoing product development.

Buy Back

Where the franchisor agrees to purchase the franchise back from the franchisee where the franchisee no longer wishes to continue.

Disclosure

The practice of revealing detailed information about the franchisor's business and franchise package, prior to the signing of the Franchise Agreement. This is a legal obligation in many European and North American countries, BUT only voluntary in the UK.

Exclusive Territory

The area within which a franchisee will operate and where they are the only person within the franchisee network that is permitted to proactively market their products or services.

Franchise Licence

The right to operate a franchise using the franchisor's brand name system of the brand, knowhow, methodology, systems, and procedures for which an initial Licence fee is charged as well as Ongoing Fees.

Franchise Contract

Often referred to as the Franchise Agreement, and sets out the terms under which the Franchise Licence is granted.

Franchise

The business format being offered for sale under a Franchise Licence.

Franchisee

The person or company buying the Franchise.

Franchise Operations Manual

The detailed document or manual which describes every aspect of how the franchisee should run their franchise business.

Franchise Package

The goods and services that the franchisor will provide a franchisee, enabling them to launch their franchise business.

Franchisor

The company selling the original Franchise and providing the support to their franchisees.

Franchisor Management Fee

Sometimes referred to as a "Royalty" or "Ongoing Fees". These are the fees that the franchisee will pay the franchisor, usually monthly, as a fixed amount or a percentage of the franchisee's turnover.

Intellectual Rights

The franchisor's "secrets" of doing business including the various Trade Marks, Patents, Branding, Manuals etc.

Master Franchise

A licence granted to an individual or company to operate in more than one territory; often Master franchises are granted for a whole Country or large Region.

P&L Projections

The calculations, based on the franchisor's experience, which predicts the franchisee's financial performance.

Pilot Operation

A test undertaken by the franchisor to assess how their franchise will operate and how successful it will be. The pilot is set-up in a separate geographic location and is run at arms distance from the franchisor to replicate how an independent franchisee should operate and perform.

Renewal

The legal provision for granting a further franchise term once the initial term has expired. Usually there are a range of conditions attached to any franchise renewal.

Re-sale

Refers to the sale of a franchise, by a franchisee, to another person or company other than the franchisor.

Royalties

Sometimes referred to as "Franchisor Management Fees" or "Ongoing Fees". These are the fees that the franchisee will pay the franchisor, usually monthly, as either a fixed amount or a percentage of the franchisee's turnover.

Term

Refers to the length of time the franchise is granted for.

Termination

The legal provision by which either party may terminate

the Franchise Agreement, often used when the franchisee materially breaches the terms of the Franchise Agreement.

Trading Act

Known as the Trading Schemes Act (1996). This was introduced to combat the maligned practice of "pyramid selling".

Vertical Block Exemption

On 1st June 2010, revised European regulation came into force effecting Vertical Agreements, which are agreements entered into by parties at different levels of the supply chain, and which includes franchising. The Vertical Block Exemption exempts franchise agreements amongst others, from being restrictive agreements under Article 101 (ex Article 81) of the EU Treaty, so long as certain conditions are met.

CHAPTER 20

Sources of help

Listed below are a selection of organisations and sites that people considering buying a franchise may find of help. Please note this is not an exhaustive list and there will be other places that there are other places where information can be found.

Selected Franchise Associations

The British Franchise Association

British Franchise Association, Centurion Court, 85f Milton Park, Abingdon, OX14 4RY

Tel: 01235 820 470

Web: www.thebfa.org

European Franchise Federation

179, ave. Louise, B-1050 Brussels, Belgium

Tel: 00 32 2 520 16 07

Web: www.eff-franchise.com

International Franchise Association

1350 New York Avenue NW #900, Washington DC 20005, USA

Tel: 001 202 628 8000

Web: www.franchise.org

For a full list of franchise associations visit:
www.thebfa.org/international.asp

Banks with Dedicated Franchise Departments

Lloyds Banking Group

Franchise Unit, 2nd Floor, Northgate House, Kingsway, Cardiff, CF10 4LD

Tel: 0800 587 2379

Web: www.lloydstsb.com/franchising

NatWest

NatWest/RBS Franchise Team, 1st Floor, 280 Bishopsgate, London, EC2M 4RB

Tel: 0800 092 917

Web: www.natwest.com/business/services/marketexpertise/franchising.ashx

The Royal Bank of Scotland plc

RBS Franchise Section, Level 1, 280 Bishopsgate, London, EC2M 4RB

Tel: 0800 092 917

Web: www.rbs.co.uk/business/banking/g3/franchising.ashx

HSBC

Franchise Unit, 12 Calthorpe Road, Birmingham, B15 1QZ

Tel: 0121 455 3438

Web: www.hsbc.co.uk

Franchise Exhibition & Show Organisers

Venture Marketing Group

Tel: 020 8394 5226

Web: www.franchiseinfo.co.uk

Prysm MFV

Tel: 0117 930 4927

Web: www.thefranchiseshow.co.uk

Job Done Marketing

Tel: 0116 242 4157

Web: www.jobdonemarketing.co.uk

Franchise Magazines

Business Franchise Magazine

6th & 7th Floor, 111 Upper Richmond Road, Putney, London, SW15 2TJ

Tel: 020 8394 5216

Franchise World

Highlands House, 165 The Broadway, Wimbledon, London, SW19 1NE

Tel: 020 8605 2555

The Franchise Magazine

Franchise House, 56 Surrey Street, Norwich, NR1 3FD

Tel: 01603 620301

What Franchise Magazine

Partridge Publications, Third Floor, Gloucester House, Gloucester Mews, South Street,

Eastbourne, East Sussex, BN21 4XH

Tel: 01323 636004

Making Money

Partridge Publications, Third Floor, Gloucester House, Gloucester Mews, South Street,

Eastbourne, East Sussex, BN21 4XH

Tel: 01323 636004

Franchise Printed Directories

FranchiseWorld Directory

Tel: 020 8605 2555

Web: www.franchiseworld.com

The United Kingdom Franchise Directory

Tel: 01603 620301

Web: www.theukfranchisedirectory.net

Newspapers that Cover Franchising

Daily Express

Daily Mail

Daily Mirror

Evening Standard

Sunday Express

The Mail on Sunday

Franchise Website Directories

Business Franchise

Tel: 020 8394 5283

Web: www.businessfranchise.com

Franchise Direct

Tel: 03531 865 6370

Web: www.franchisedirect.co.uk

Franchise World

Tel: 020 8605

Web: www.franchiseworld.com

Making Money

Tel: 01323 636000

Web: www.makingmoney.com

Selectyourfranchise

Tel: 023 8027 5710

Web: www.selctyourfranchise.com

What Franchise

Tel: 01323 636000

Web: www.whatfranchisemagazine.co.uk

Whichfranchise.com

Tel: 0141 204 0050

Web: www.whichfranchise.com

CHAPTER 21

Encouraging women into franchising (EWIF)

EWIF is an exciting organisation dedicated to encouraging women into franchising. EWIF is a not-for-profit organisation, run by volunteers from within the industry. Its members come from all areas within the franchising industry and include: Franchisors, Franchisees, Banks, Consultants, Accountants, Solicitors, Media Providers, Exhibition Organisers, as well as other associated businesses.

The remit of EWIF is three fold and simple;

1. To encourage women to consider buying a franchise operation
2. To encourage women with existing businesses to franchise them
3. To help existing franchisors to attract more women into their franchise

EWIF offers a range of FREE services including:

- Half hour free telephone support and advice
- Mentoring

EWIF members also undertake:

- Public speaking
- Providing case studies
- Media interviews
- Attendance at Franchise events

EWIF also hold an annual Awards event recognising the work of women in all aspects of the world of franchising.

For information about the work of EWIF please visit www.ewif.org

EWIF
encouraging women
into franchising

The *Mission* of the group:

The EWIF group is dedicated to encouraging woman into franchising. Its members come from all areas of the franchise industry and include: Franchisors, Franchisees, Banks, Consultants, Accountants, Solicitors, Media Providers, Exhibition Organisers, as well as other associated businesses.

3 target groups:

1 Women looking to become franchisees	*2* Women business owners looking to expand through franchising	*3* Existing Franchisors that have businesses suitable for woman franchisees

EWIF's mission is to inspire, encourage, educate and support women considering or involved in franchising through its network of Ambassadors.

info@ewif.org | www.ewif.org
Inspire | Educate | Encourage | Support

CHAPTER 22

Author profiles

CLIVE SAWYER

Managing Director, Business Options
Founder & Director, Encouraging Women into Franchising (EWIF)

Clive is the Managing Director of Business Options, a specialist franchise and business expansion consultancy. Business Options is the only Franchise Consultancy in the UK that is accredited by all of the following: The British Franchise Association, The Irish Franchise Association, and The Institute of Business Consulting. This ensures that we have the breadth of skills, knowledge and experience to develop the most suitable franchise models for our clients that meets their needs as the franchisor and the future franchisees.

The team at Business Options has over twenty years experience within the Franchising sector. Our experience reflects that we have worked with many different businesses in many different sectors both domestically and internationally. We regularly run franchising seminars for the British Franchise Association and the leading Franchise Banks.

Clive Sawyer, Managing Director of Business Options is also a renowned franchising expert and writes articles for the leading franchise magazines as well as being a multi published author on franchising in the UK.

Clive is also founder and a director of the Encouraging Women into Franchising Group (EWIF), which provides advice and guidance to women looking to enter the world of franchising whether as a franchisee or as a business owner looking to franchise their business.

Contact
Tel: 01420 550890
Email: clive.sawyer@businessoptions.biz
Web: www.businessoptions.biz

MURIELLE MAUPOINT

Managing Director, LiveIt Ventures
Director, Encouraging Women into Franchising (EWIF)

Murielle Maupoint is the Founder of Live It Ventures, an inspirational business built on the simple philosophy that everyone has a purpose to fulfill – a legacy that lasts long after they are gone. A life other than this is a life not lived to the full. Live It empowers ordinary people who have an extraordinary passion, purpose and desire to make a difference through what they do . . . Entrepreneurs, Solopreneurs and Business Owners with big ideas that could change the world if not their own lives; Unknown Authors dreaming of their books being published to capture the imagination of a new generation; Individuals and Organisations with the vision to make an impact wherever and whenever they can . . .

Murielle's expertise in business and psychology has taken her on her own amazing journey, which has involved working with some of the most disadvantaged and dysfunctional people in society to the most privileged. Having also been the Chief Executive of an award winning organisation she now coaches and mentors entrepreneurs, business professionals and Executives. Murielle holds a BSc (Hons) Psychology, an MBA and a range of top certifications in NLP Coaching amongst others. As a practicing Psychologist, a Social Entrepreneur, a Business Expansion Consultant, leading Trainer of NLP and highly sought after motivational speaker, Murielle is totally dedicated to enabling others to be the best that they can be.

Murielle is founding member and a director of Encouraging Women into Franchising (EWIF), which provides advice and guidance to women who want to invest in a franchise and business owners who want to franchise their business.

If you would like to benefit from Murielle's expertise and passion then please get in touch with her using the details below:

Contact
Tel: 0845 388 1128
Email: yourlife@liveit.com
Web: www.liveit.com

Live with Passion
Fulfill your Purpose
Connect for Success
Leave a Legacy

Inspiring you to live your life!

If you were 100% certain of success...

What would you do right now that you are not doing?

How would you choose to live your life?

Unlock your potential with Live It...

We are ready to inspire you to live your life.

Contact us now for more information:

www.liveit.com 0845 388 1128

How can you create a life that is truly extraordinary?

What would be possible if you could?

A GUIDE TO LIVING ON PURPOSE WITH MEANING AND FREEDOM

In this extraordinarily helpful guide Ian Lock takes you through the ideas, insights and explorations that will lead you to answer these questions and more. The ambition here is no less than to have you 'own and live the life you want'. So be prepared to be provoked and challenged. And get ready to shift your thinking and belief.

Recognised as a brilliant coach and consultant, Ian Lock is a guide you can trust. Let him take you on an exploration into what matters to you and how you can get more of what you care about.

'There are very few books that do what they say they do! This is a powerful guide to anyone who wants more from their life - read it! Go on and be extraordinary!"
Anni Townend, Author of *Assertiveness and Diversity*

ISBN: 978-1-906954-70-3
Published: 3 January 2013
Format: Paperback
RRP: £12.99

DEVASTATED BY REDUNDANCY?

LEARN HOW TO USE THIS OPPORTUNITY TO CREATE A NEW AND BETTER LIFE FOR YOURSELF...

If you're one of the millions either already - or about to be - affected by redundancy, this book is for you.

It will enable you to:

- walk away from negative feelings of loss, despair, sadness;
- Understand that your occupational identity may be a thing of the past, but your unique identity isn't;
- Find the resources you need in this time of transition;
- Identify your new niche in life; and
- Develop positive and powerful ways of achieving it.

'This book is the next best thing to being coached by Elaine. On Masterchef, contestants sometimes say "That's me on a plate". This is Elaine in a book: warm, wise and witty. Best of all, parts of the book are laugh out loud funny - and I wasn't expecting that.'
Redundancy coaching client

ISBN: 978-1-906954-55-0
Published: 16 October 2012

Format: Paperback
RRP: £18.99

Despite following the advice of a wealth of best-selling self-help books, most of us still struggle to understand the fundamental laws and principles that govern the universe, our interactions within it and our ability to achieve success, health, wealth and happiness.

Have you ever wondered why the Law of Attraction doesn't work for you?

The answer is simple: The Universal Laws <u>cannot</u> *work in your favour until you identify and remove the psychological issues that are blocking your ability to live the life you want.*

In her ground breaking and easy-to-understand book, psychotherapist Deborah Sless, uses the concrete psychological theory of Transactional Analysis to uncover the secrets of the Universal Laws. **Beyond Our Illusions** takes you on a journey of self-discovery to understand:

- The Universal Laws and how they impact our lives
- Your own individual Life Story and the beliefs that were formed in childhood
- How to achieve freedom from your illusions and master your self
- The concept of Spirit as an energy force and how to tap into it

Genuine self-development is not easy but Deborah Sless provides her readers with the tools and framework they need - through clear explanations, examples and exercises - to begin a journey of self-discovery and change toward ultimate fulfilment.

ISBN: 978-1-906954-42-0
Publication: 1 August 2012

Format: Paperback
RRP: £14.99